BEVERLEY HARE started teaching assertiveness training in 1984 for government departments and adult educational institutions in Australia. She returned to Britain in 1986 and continued this work until 1988 when she took up a full-time training position with a large financial institution in Sussex.

She has now returned to freelance training, specialising in Assertiveness and Stress Management. This work takes her all over the country but she has made her home in Sussex.

This is her first book.

D1375257

BE ASSERTIVE

The positive way to communicate effectively

Beverley Hare

VERMILION
LONDON

· First published by Optima in 1988

Reprinted 1990, 1992, 1994

1 3 5 7 9 10 8 6 4 2

This revised edition published in the United Kingdom in 1996 by Vermilion an imprint of Ebury Press

Random House UK Ltd
Random House
20 Vauxhall Bridge Road
London SW1V 2SA

Random House Australia (Pty) Ltd
20 Alfred Street, Milsons Point, Sydney,
New South Wales 2061, Australia

Random House New Zealand Limited
18 Poland Road, Glenfield,
Auckland 10, New Zealand

Random House, South Africa (Pty) Limited
Box 2263, Rosebank 2121, South Africa

Random House UK Limited Reg. No. 954009

A CIP catalogue record for this book is available from the British Library.

ISBN 0 09 181396 4

Printed and bound in Great Britain by Mackays of Chatham, plc

Papers used by Vermilion are natural, recyclable products made from wood grown in sustainable forests.

CONTENTS

ACKNOWLEDGMENTS

I would first and foremost like to thank my cousin and dear friend Penny Pilch, without whom this book would not have been written. She greeted my first tentative thoughts about writing a book with enthusiasm, put me in touch with Optima, encouraged me when my fears caused me to want to abandon the idea, and read the manuscript, offering both constructive comments to improve it and positive feedback about what it contained.

My thanks also go to my friend Hilary Greaves, who read the manuscript and gave a great deal of thought and consideration to what it contained. She was enthusiastic about the book and suggestions she made for change or amplification were sensitively given and gratefully received.

Special thanks are due to my mother Pat Hare, who typed the first draft, suggested changes, and has had the openness of mind to take the ideas in the book and use them in her own life.

Finally, thanks to my family, friends and students, both here and in Australia, for their part in the making of this book – and their contribution to my development as a person.

Ferring, West Sussex
December 1987

INTRODUCTION

WHO I WAS ELEVEN YEARS AGO

In September 1976 I left my marriage of seven years. It was one of the first major decisions I had made in my life and set me off on a path of change and self-development which still continues today. At that time I was a very passive, dependent and, for the most part, non-assertive person. During the years of my marriage I had allowed what spirit I had to be squashed and when I left I felt I was a person with no identity of my own. To a large extent I had become a 'yes' person. From a need to be liked and approved of by others, particularly my husband, I had lost touch with who I was, what I wanted and how I felt. It is not surprising that I thought of myself as a person with no identity.

I would like to make it clear at this point, that I am in no way implying that my husband was responsible for the way I was at that time. It will become apparent as you read this book that taking responsibility for feelings, thoughts, beliefs and choices, is part of what it means to be assertive – and I take full responsibility for where I found myself at that time. I chose a man who I perceived as someone I could lean on, who would take care of me and make the decisions. I handed over the responsibility for my life and happiness to another person. I was virtually saying, 'You lead my life for me. I don't want to take the responsibility for leading it myself'. I did not realize the price I would have to pay in terms of loss of 'self', and I got exactly what I wanted. Of course, for his part, he also got what he wanted. He wanted a passive, dependent, non-assertive wife – someone he could mould, take care of, dominate and control. We had made our choices – neither of us were 'victims'.

Today I look back on my marriage without regret. It

was a very important learning experience for me. For
the first couple of years I was happy in a very
turbulent, passionate sort of way. Then, as I handed
over more and more of my 'self' to him, life began to
feel empty and meaningless. I tried to run away from
the pain because I was terrified of facing up to the
reality of my situation. I had been brought up as a
Catholic and divorce was not an acceptable part of my
personal reality. I was afraid of being alone, I was
afraid of hurting him and I was afraid of being a
failure. In my attempt to escape from myself and my
fear and pain, I started drinking, I tried smoking
marijuana, I took anti-depressants and tranquillizers.
Luckily I hated the feeling of being out-of-control and
this period was very brief. Then I faced reality – I was
desperately unhappy and could not continue the way I
was going. I felt the choice was between my sanity and
my marriage – I chose sanity.

I left him for a week when we were living in Canada
but he persuaded me to return to Australia with him
and give our marriage one last try in a settled
environment. I agreed. It was a very constructive step
for me to take. In Australia I had a very close and dear
friend who also had marital problems. For the first
time in all the tumult I had someone I could talk to
openly and freely. I took up yoga which helped to
stabilize me. I was now facing up to my problems
instead of running away from them. Six months after
my return to Australia I had the strength and courage
to leave my marriage and start a new life alone.

WHO I AM TODAY

Today I am a very different person. In fact when I
think of who I was at that time, I find it difficult to
believe that the 'me' I am now inhabits the same body
as the 'me' I was then. The change has not been an
easy one. It has required a great deal of effort, self-
examination, risk-taking and pain. However, the pain
of personal development is a far different animal to

that of the pain of repression and avoidance. On the other side of the pain of personal development is more fun, more laughter, more spontaneity, more experiences, more love, more joy, more acceptance and more understanding. Here pain equals gain. On the other side of the pain of repression and avoidance is less fun, less laughter, less spontaneity, fewer experiences, less love, less joy, less acceptance and less understanding. Here pain equals loss. The pain involved in personal development has been worthwhile for me, because at the other side of it I have always gained by becoming more of what I am capable of being.

I remember asking the Director of an organisation I was doing counselling training with, 'How long did it take you to get "there"?' He laughed and replied, 'I'm not "there". No such place exists. I expect to continue developing all through my life.' I had thought I could do a few courses and become perfect! Now I know it is a lifelong process. I have learned a great deal, I continue to learn with every experience I encounter, and I hope I shall never think that I have got 'there'. If I do, it will mean that I am stagnating – I will have given up doing what I believe life is all about – becoming *all* that I am capable of being.

Back to who I am today. I am now an active, independent and, for the most part, assertive person. I also happen to teach assertiveness training courses and have done so for the past four years. What follows in this book are the major areas I cover in my courses. I have illustrated the points I am making with examples from my own life. I have chosen to use personal examples rather than case studies because communicating about myself is what assertiveness is all about and I think it is important for me to practise what I preach. I have had to learn what I teach and I shall share with you my mistakes and failures, as well as my successes. I hope that by doing so the book will have more meaning for you and help you to become all that *you* are capable of being.

11

WHY I AM WRITING THIS BOOK

In September 1986 I returned to England after having spent the previous ten years in Sydney, Australia. For the last two and a half years of my time there I had been teaching assertivness training for various adult education organisations and government departments. From my observations of the status of assertiveness training in Britain, it appears that it is seen as something which is relevant to women but not to men. This had also been the case in Australia at one time, but has changed in the last few years to the extent where I regularly taught courses where the participants were either all men or predominantly men. It is my belief that a world where *both* men and women were able to be assertive would be a better world. I would certainly prefer to have people in my life who know how to express themselves assertively – men and women. Unfortunately, there are many misconceptions about what communicating assertively involves. Often people think they are behaving assertively when they are behaving aggressively. To add to this confusion some of the books available on assertion present a view of it which is also quite aggressive.

My main purpose in writing this book is to address both men and women and to present assertion as an effective form of communication, which promotes honest, open relationships in any area of your life in which you are prepared to use the skills. I do not believe, however, that a book is a substitute for taking a course and recommend that, if you find this book interesting and believe assertion could be a valuable skill for you to learn, that you take an assertiveness training course. Whilst I cannot claim that the ideas presented in this book are original (they are the result of reading many books, attending numerous courses in personal development, and teaching hundreds of students) they do have my own personal stamp on them. I, like you, am a unique human being and the way in which I present and interpret ideas and experiences is my own original way. I hope it will be of use to you.

1.
ASSERTION, AGGRESSION OR NON-ASSERTION?

Assertion is not a character trait with which some people come into this world and others do not. It is a communication skill and, like any other skill, can be learned. In order to learn it you must know what it is and be able to distinguish it from aggression and non-assertion. You will probably recognize yourself as being aggressive, assertive and non-assertive at different times. With some people you may find yourself behaving like a 'wimp', afraid to speak up for yourself. With others you may find you play the 'heavy', trampling on their feelings and rights. And with some you may be able to express yourself honestly and openly in a calm and respectful way. But it is likely that you will find one of these modes of behaviour predominates.

There is no such thing as a 100 per cent assertive person – I am certainly not a 100 per cent assertive person. At one time in my life, I would say my behaviour was non-assertive most of the time, with an occasional burst into open aggression and rare dash of assertion. Now I usually engage in assertive behaviour,

I occasionally behave aggressively, and when I am being non-assertive it is more often than not from choice.

CHOOSING YOUR BEHAVIOUR

When attending an assertion training class or reading books on assertion, it is important to remember that you can choose how you want to behave. Learning to be assertive does not mean that in order to be a successful student you must behave assertively at all times in all situations. What can be gained through raising your awareness of the differences between assertion, non-assertion and aggression and learning the skills involved in being assertive is that you can gradually start to *choose* how you want to behave in certain situations. I say 'gradually' because it takes time and effort to change behaviour. You will not finish this book or an assertion course and be a reformed personality. I participated in my first assertion course nine years ago and there are still situations where I have not chosen how I behave.

I would like to define what I mean when I use the word *choice* in this chapter. When I say there are still situations where I do not choose my own behaviour, I mean the type of situation where I would like to have behaved differently and came away thinking, 'If only I had said . . . . .', or, 'I wish I had said . . . . .'. There are a number of reasons why I do not behave assertively in these types of situations. One of the major inhibiting factors for me is fear. For example, if I tell my friend that I am angry with her maybe she will be angry, or scornful or hurt. I fear her anger, or scorn or hurt because of the way I think I will feel if she reacts in that way. But it is important for me to take responsibility for my fear of her reaction rather than to blame her for it. In another situation, I may feel so angry with a person that I hold it inside rather than express it, because I am afraid of what will happen if I actually let it out – I may get out of control and physically or verbally attack the other person. It is difficult to be assertive if you feel excessive anger (this will be discussed further in Chapter 11). In another situation, I may want to tell someone that I love them but I am afraid of being rejected.

There is a distinct difference between *reacting* and *choosing*. I am reacting when I would like to have done it differently. I am choosing when I say to myself, 'I know this person is trying to put me down, but I do not choose to say anything about it at this time because . . . . .' You choose when you have weighed up the situation, looked at the possible outcomes of making an assertive statement, and come to the conclusion that it is or is not worth it. You may be thinking that things often happen very fast and there is not time to go through all this before making a response. This is true but as you try out assertion skills and gradually become more assertive you will find that you start to respond assertively as a natural response. For example, at one time it was difficult for me to refuse a request of a friend. Once I learned about assertion I gradually became more comfortable saying no, and now the situations I would once have agonized over hardly cost me a thought. Most times I say no if I do not want to do something, and yes if I do.

However, we humans can be very tricky at times and fool ourselves. We can appear to be very logical in our reasoning about a particular situation, when really we are terrified and are covering up our fear with rationalizations. I know – I have done it myself often! I remember a time when I justified not taking assertive action in a work situation to a friend. I came up with some very logical reasons for not being assertive, but later realized that the real issue was that I was afraid. When I told my friend the real reason for my decision to be non-assertive, she was amazed. She said, 'But you were so logical and reasonable that I was totally convinced by your arguments.' Of course she was. The person I had most needed to convince was myself and I came up with some very good arguments. It is quite reasonable to choose not to assert yourself because you are afraid – the problem arises when you deny your fear and pretend there are other reasons for your decision. Beware of logic and reason! They can be very useful in many areas of our lives – but can also be our enemies with respect to honesty about our feelings.

ASSERTION

'Assertion has been defined as standing up for personal rights and expressing thoughts, feelings and beliefs in direct, honest and appropriate ways which do not violate another person's rights.' (A.J. Lange and P. Jakubowski, *Responsible Assertive Behavior: Cognitive/ Behavioral Procedures for Trainers*, Research Press, Illinois, 1976)

When I am being assertive, I express who I am. I tell you what I think, how I feel and what I believe. I do so in a direct and honest way, which is also appropriate. What is meant by appropriate? I may walk into a room and take a dislike towards you on sight. It might be direct and honest of me to say, 'I don't like your face', but it is hardly appropriate!

What does it mean 'not to violate another person's rights?' I will discuss personal rights in detail in Chapter 9 but, for the present, it is necessary to say that one most important right is the right to be treated with respect. It is also important to be aware that personal rights apply to both myself and other people. A useful indicator of whether you are violating another person's rights is to ask yourself, 'Would I like to be spoken to or treated in the way I am treating this person?'

When I am being assertive I express myself, but I do so in a way which is both *'self'* and *'other'* enhancing. I maintain my self-respect and I treat you with respect. It is an interaction between equals. I do not involve myself in putdowns nor do I try to dominate you. In assertion the aim is for a win-win situation – I approach you as a person who has a right to be treated with respect; I express what I want to say and take responsibility for my words; I allow you the courtesy of expressing what you want to say. Assertive communication is a two-way process – I communicate with you and give you the space to communicate with me. You then decide whether or not you wish to communicate with me – it is your choice.

NON-ASSERTION

'Non-assertion involves violating one's own rights by failing to express honest feelings, thoughts and beliefs, and consequently permitting others to violate oneself.' (A.J. Lange and P. Jakubowski, *Responsible Assertive Behavior: Cognitive/Behavioral Procedures for Trainers*, Research Press, Illinois, 1976)

One of the assertive personal rights is the right to express myself – my feelings, thoughts and beliefs. By not taking on this right, a person will allow themselves to be walked over, taken for granted and treated without respect. A crucial part of this definition is that it places responsibility very firmly at the feet of the person who is behaving non-assertively. It is my responsibility if I allow people to violate my rights, if I allow myself to be walked over and if I allow myself to be taken for granted.

Sometimes the emphasis on responsibility in assertion can seem like a heavy load to carry when people first come into contact with the idea. It is so much more comfortable to rant and rave about how awful people are and how badly they treat you – 'The world would be a wonderful place if it were not for all the people out there who victimize me and make my life a misery!' It often seems easier to blame others than to take responsibility for your life. Taking responsibility has its benefits – benefits which far outweigh any deficits you may perceive. If I take responsibility for my feelings, I can change them. If I decide someone else is responsible for my feelings, I cannot change them. If I feel angry every time you

leave dishes in the sink and I make you responsible for
my feelings of anger, I give you tremendous power.
You can make me angry any time you like – you have
control of my emotions! If I take the responsibility
myself, I can then do something about the feeling of
anger. It is mine – I own it. I can express it – or not
express it. I can change it – or not change it.

Sometimes people think they are behaving
assertively and do not understand why they are not
taken seriously. The problem is that you may be saying
assertive words, but doing so in a way which makes it
easy for others to disregard them. If I approach some
one in a self-effacing and apologetic manner,
whispering the words and looking at the floor, it is
highly unlikely that they will take me seriously. An
assertive message needs to have some impact behind it.
I need to believe I have the right to express myself and
to back my words up with appropriate non-verbal
behaviour – for example, firm tone of voice, direct eye
contact and upright posture.

If you are a person who behaves non-assertively a lot
of the time, it might be useful for you to look at the
reasons behind your behaviour. This behaviour often
arises from a desire to avoid conflict and to please
other people. Ask yourself if you *need* people to like
you. There is absolutely nothing wrong with wanting
to be liked – it feels good. However, there is a big
difference between *needing* to be liked and *wanting* to
be liked. If I need your love and approval I will be
prepared to do cartwheels for it. If I want your love and
approval I may feel saddened or a bit anxious when I
do not get it, but I will not be devastated. I will not
have to run around trying to get back in favour again
in order to be acceptable to you. Self-esteem is an
important aspect in the way we behave. As a person's
self-esteem increases their *need* to be liked and
approved of changes to a *want*. The reason for this is
that if I can value myself highly I will not be in such
need for you to value me highly. You may disapprove
of me but my self-esteem rests, not in your hands, but

in mine.

The predominantly non-assertive person needs to reclaim the power which they have given away. The word *power* often conjures up uncomfortable images in people's minds. It did in mine when I first came across it in this sense. The reason for this is that I thought of it in terms of *power over* someone else. If I have power over you it implies I can control you. This idea sat very uneasily with me. The power I am talking about is *personal power*. When I take responsibility for my feelings, thoughts, beliefs, actions and life, then I start to reclaim my personal power. For example, at times I used to feel that my husband did not care about me, because he would do something that I did not like. Of course, I had not told him I did not like it because 'if he loved me he would know how I feel'! This was in the days when I thought people were mindreaders. I have since discovered that most people are not in the business of reading minds and if you want them either to do or not to do something, then you need to tell them about it. They may decide not to meet your needs, but you have more chance than if you do not ask for what you want. I could have changed the situation by the use of personal power. If I had taken responsibility for my feelings of upset instead of making him responsible, I could then have made a decision about what to do to change it. Instead, I felt victimized and powerless and nothing changed.

AGGRESSION

'Aggression involves directly standing up for personal rights and expressing thoughts, feelings and beliefs in a way which is often dishonest, usually inappropriate, and always violates the rights of the other person.' (A.J. Lange and P. Jakubowski, *Responsible Assertive Behavior: Cognitive/Behavioral Procedures for Trainers*, Research Press, Illinois, 1976).

You may be wondering how aggression falls into the category of often being dishonest. People I have known who tend to behave aggressively often say, 'But I just said what I thought – I was only being honest'. Where aggression becomes dishonest is that, unlike assertion where personal responsibility is taken for feelings and thoughts, in aggression the person often abdicates responsibility. For example, a person may say, 'You were wrong to talk to me in that tone of voice'. The person has said what they thought. The reason it is dishonest is that the person sending the message has said nothing about themselves or their feelings about the situation. The whole message is focused away from the sender onto the receiver. The concentration is on the receiver and his or her shortcomings. In an assertive message the concentration is on the sender and how they feel. This aspect of assertion will become clearer when we talk about 'I' messages in Chapter 5.

Aggression sets up a win/lose situation. I am going to win and you are going to lose. I am right and you are wrong! The following aggressive messages show the win/lose aspect:

- 'This is what I think – you're stupid if you think otherwise.'
- 'This is what I want – what you want isn't important.'
- 'This is what I feel – your feelings don't matter.'

These are the underlying messages of many aggressive communications, although they may not be spoken openly in this way. For example, I was talking about politics with someone recently and his response to a view I expressed was, 'Surely you don't believe that rubbish'. His statement implied, 'I think it is rubbish – you're stupid if you think otherwise'.

We have all learned ways to cope with our environment and the people we meet in it. As a child we may have learned that the way to get by was to be placating and keep the peace at all costs. Or, we may have learned that unless we came on as a big 'heavy'

no-one took any notice of us. A few fortunates may
have been encouraged to express themselves and been
treated with respect when they did so. However, we are
not condemned in adult life to continuing using the
coping mechanisms we had as children. We all have
the capacity to change – if we choose to do so. Books
and courses may help, but will not do it for us. The
crucial element involved in changing is *you* or *me*. You
must provide the impetus of motivation and desire.
Change of any kind involves being prepared to take
risks and this is what I shall discuss in the next
chapter.

2.
CHANGE –
THE RISK
FACTOR

One of the things that happens as you change your
behaviour is that the people around you react to the
change. We are creatures of habit. We like things the
way they are. We like to be able to predict how our
nearest and dearest will behave. We have got used to
them the way they are and there is a certain comfort
in that familiarity. We are even comfortable with
negative behaviour in a perverse sort of way. I know
that as I have changed I have received encouragement
from some and opposition from others. From the same
person I have received encouragement over some
changes and opposition to other changes. People can
become threatened by change in others for many
different reasons. It is not so important to ask why
others oppose changes in your behaviour, but more
important to ask yourself, 'How am I going to cope
with it?' It is a trap to focus on the other person. What
we need to do is to look at ourselves. The way in which
we change, develop and grow, is by looking at our own
behaviour and emotions, not at other people's.

I will look for a moment at the desire most of us
have to change other people. We tend to think, 'If only
she were more open, I would be able to communicate
with her honestly', or, 'If he were more reasonable we
would not have so much conflict in the home'. I can tell
you most confidently that you will never change
another person – the only person you can change is

yourself! The paradoxical part of this is that if you change yourself you will find others changing around you. Gain more respect for yourself – and you will find others have more respect for you. Believe you are intelligent – and others will treat you as an intelligent person whose opinion is worth hearing. Feel attractive – and others will find you attractive.

Does it all sound too easy? I can assure you it is not. Despite this it is well worth any discomfort or pain you may experience along the way. Changing requires effort, practice, courage, honesty and determination. It may appear as if I am setting up a very negative picture – perhaps it is even putting you off starting on the path of change. My reason for talking about the difficulties involved is that I prefer to deal with reality and not paint a picture of change as something that is full of joy, ease and light. I would not be being honest with you if I did that. My own path of change has been difficult and painful, and at times I have questioned whether it is all worth it.

I do believe that change at a deep and meaningful level is painful. Many of the books I have read on various areas of personal development (books from which I have gained a great deal) talk about change as if it were an easy, painless process. They give the impression that you just need to follow their advice and in no time at all you will be just the way you want to be! From my own experience and that of people I have known who have involved themselves in personal development, change is painful. The problem with starting out believing that it will all be easy is that at the first obstacle you are likely to say to yourself, 'It does not work. I am giving up'. When I hit my first major obstacle that is exactly what I wanted to do. I was able to talk it through with someone who gave me encouragement and support. I am delighted that I decided to continue. I would not like to have stayed the person I was then – I would have missed out on a lot of life and living.

I believe that the most difficult person for us to face

is *ourselves* and in changing, that is who we are up against. It is important to realize and understand that in changing a great deal of resistance comes from within ourselves. Whilst we may think we want to change, part of us fights that change, and this can bring about feelings of depression and a desire to give up and run away from ourselves. We are masters at disassociating from our selves. I do not want to go into the complexities of how we do it, but a useful guide to self-awareness is to treat the people in your life as a mirror. If you dislike something about a friend, ask yourself if you have that trait in yourself. It is not all negative – also look at the things you like about others and you may find they are also in you. They may not be fully developed, but perhaps you will surprise yourself! If you meet with opposition and criticism from others as you change, it is also useful to ask yourself if there is a little critical or opposing voice in yourself which a friend or relative is mirroring.

When I was trying to change my behaviour with men and place my relationships on a more equal footing by taking men's phone numbers when they took mine and phoning them if I chose to, I felt some disapproval from women friends. At first I focused on them and their 'shortcomings'. After a while I realized that they were only mirroring my own internal critic and while I was looking at them and what I disliked I was not dealing with the real issue. The real issue was that I had been socialized as a woman and there were messages going around in my head about how 'real' women *should* behave. I discovered messages like – 'Don't chase men', 'Play hard to get', 'It's not feminine', 'I am supposed to do the waiting'. Once I discovered this, real change started to occur with the result that my relationships with men are far more equal today. I should add that opposition did not only come from women but also from men. Men have been socialized too and have their own set of messages which make it difficult for them to accept women taking a more active role in relationships. Fortunately things are changing and in my observations of younger people it appears that in many cases they have more equal relationships with sex roles becoming less rigidly defined. Many of us who have been conditioned into rigid sex roles are breaking out of them and becoming freer in the way we relate to each other.

The deficits of change can be seen as pain and difficulties along the way. It can create relationship problems when others do not want us to change. Of course, it is always possible to change our perception of what a problem is. I now see problems as challenges to be overcome. They are something along the way that can help me to develop and become stronger. They are not something which defeats me and which I add to the list of life's burdens to be tolerated.

As far as I am concerned the benefits of change far outweigh the deficits. Perhaps I can best explain the benefits in terms of the changes I have made:

1976	1987
Low self-esteem	Improved self-esteem
Little self-confidence	Improved self-confidence
Believed I was unintelligent	Believe I am intelligent
Believed I was unattractive	More belief in my attractiveness
Terrified of speaking in groups	Very comfortable speaking in groups

1976	1987
Dependent	More independent
Passive	More active
Predominantly non-assertive	Predominantly assertive
Obsessive, dependent relationships with men	Relationships with men more interdependent
Sensitive to criticism	Handle criticism well, even when it hurts
Worked as a secretary	Work as teacher/consultant

I do not wish to imply from the above that I am 'there'. As I said in the Introduction 'there' is non-existent. I am trying to show you that 11 years ago I was a very different person to the one I am today – and I much prefer who I am today. All the areas in the 1987 column can be improved upon – and there are areas not mentioned that I am putting a great deal of energy into at the moment. I could still be the person in the 1976 column if I had not been prepared to take the risks and face the pain and difficulties involved in changing. The question I ask you is, 'Who would you rather be if you were me?'. Perhaps your decision as to whether *you* want to change or not will lie in your answer.

3.
RESPONSIBILITY AND BLAME

I have talked about the necessity of taking responsibility if one is to behave assertively. I need now to make a distinction between *blame* and *responsibility* and explain what I mean when I use these words.

I take responsibility when I *own* my feelings, thoughts, beliefs and actions. In expressing this ownership I would say – I feel, I think, I believe. In taking responsibility for my actions I claim them as my own as well. For example, you are not responsible for the fact that I screamed at you when you behaved aggressively towards me. I am. Your aggressive behaviour may have triggered off a response from me, but you did not make me scream. I could have chosen many different reactions. I could have walked away, cried, laughed, become silent, or even expressed calmly how I felt about your behaviour. However, I *chose* to scream and I am responsible for my own behaviour.

You may feel that in these types of situations you have not chosen your behaviour and using choice as defined in Chapter 1 (see page 16), you may not have. The problem is that we automatically use patterns of behaviour we have learned which are not particularly useful or constructive. We often have a 'knee jerk' reaction to situations. You behave aggressively – I scream back. It is hardly your fault or responsibility that I have chosen this way to react.

I am using 'choice' in a slightly different way here and would like to explain myself further. The fact is

31

that however we behave, we have made a decision at
some point in our lives that this is the way to deal
with these types of situations. I may have decided
when I was five that the way to deal with other
children who behave aggressively is to scream at them
– it may even have been quite effective. The trouble is
that we get stuck in a groove and carry on using
behaviours like this when they are no longer useful or
appropriate. Sometimes it may be appropriate to meet
aggression with screaming – if you are being attacked
in the street it might be a good idea to scream like
hell! In many instances, however, it is neither useful
nor constructive. It is beneficial to you to take
responsibility for your behaviour. Once you say to
yourself, 'I am totally responsible for my reaction to
this situation', then you can look at making changes.
You can try out other ways of handling people who
behave aggressively towards you.

Sometimes it is necessary and appropriate to ask
other people to take responsibility for their actions. Say
you are a supervisor at work and one of your staff has
made an error in a report which has had serious
repercussions. Your staff member is obviously
responsible for his or her actions and it is appropriate
that they take *responsibility*. What often happens in
this type of situation is that the supervisor goes a step
further than asking the staff member to take
responsibility and *blames* them. There is a distinct
difference in assertion between 'blame' and
'responsibility'. I will explain how blame works and
how it leads to aggressive or non-assertive behaviour. I
will also show how taking responsibility leads to
assertive behaviour.

BLAME AND AGGRESSION

*EVENT . . . BLAME OTHER PERSON . . . ANGER
. . . FRUSTRATION . . . AGGRESSION*

Looking at the process as shown above, an event occurs and I blame the other person. I may say things to myself like, 'That was a really rotten thing to do' or 'What a stupid woman to say that'. As I say these types of things to myself, I am likely to get angrier and angrier. I will feel frustrated – after all, if the other person were not so rotten or stupid I would not be feeling like this. I am likely to feel indignant and self-righteous. My behaviour will be aggressive and I will attack the other person in some way – maybe physically, maybe verbally.

BLAME AND NON-ASSERTION

EVENT . . . BLAME SELF . . . SELF-CONSCIOUS AND EMBARRASSED . . . LOW SELF-ESTEEM . . . NON-ASSERTION

In this case, an event occurs and rather than blaming the other person, I blame myself. I give myself a hard time. I am likely to be saying things to myself like, 'It's all my fault', 'I shouldn't have said that', 'I've done it again' or 'I'm so hopeless'. I will feel self-conscious and embarrassed, my self-esteem will go down, and my behaviour will be non-assertive. If I give myself a bad time about something, my self-esteem has nowhere to go but down – it will not remain the same and it certainly will not go up. It is difficult to be assertive if you are feeling bad about yourself.

RESPONSIBILITY AND ASSERTION

EVENT . . . NO BLAME . . . RESPONSIBILITY . . . CONSTRUCTIVE CONCERN . . . POSITIVE FEELINGS . . . ASSERTION

Following the above line to assertive behaviour, an event happens and there is no blame. I do not give you a hard time and I do not give myself a hard time. I do take responsibility for my feelings, thoughts, beliefs and actions. I will look at the situation and how it can best be handled rather than focusing on personalities – yours or mine. My concern will be constructive – I will try to solve the problem, not find a scapegoat. I will feel positive about dealing with the situation and my behaviour will be assertive.

PASSIVE-AGGRESSION

EVENT ... BLAME ... OTHER PERSON ... ANGER ... FRUSTRATION ... FEELINGS NOT EXPRESSED ... PASSIVE-AGGRESSION

There is a fourth type of behaviour I would like to discuss, which is perhaps the most destructive of all. If you follow the line towards aggression but imagine that the aggression is not openly expressed, you have passive-aggression. This type of aggression is covert, whereas open aggression is overt. Overt aggression is something you are usually aware of. It is the punch in the face, the screaming voice, the glaring eyes, the cold deathly quiet voice or the sarcastic comment. Overt aggression comes over in a number of ways but it is usually fairly obvious. In contrast, passive-aggression is hidden – it is what I call 'under the table stuff'. You do not really know what is going on, but you may have the very uncomfortable feeling that someone is having a go at you. Sometimes you might be being a bit over-sensitive and paranoid – we can all be paranoid at times – but very often what is happening is that the person *is* having a go at you. They are being passive-aggressive. What this arises from on many occasions is the person goes through *event ... blame other person ... anger ... frustration*, but they do not express it. The feelings get squashed and come out in distorted ways.

Because at one time my pattern was not to express myself directly, I would sometimes engage in passive-aggression. An example of this was an evening when I was waiting for a friend to come to dinner and he arrived 45 minutes late. I was very angry but as I walked from the lounge to the front door I talked myself out of saying anything. 'Don't cause a fuss', 'Don't be so intolerant', 'Don't upset the evening by being angry', were the kinds of messages I said to myself. As a consequence I did not express my feelings to him. The result was that an hour or so later I found myself having a dig at him. As soon as I did it I realized what I had done, but many people are not very aware of their own behaviour and will be passive-aggressive and not realize it.

Passive-aggression can come out almost immediately – as mine did – or it can come out much later and at times seem quite unrelated to the original event. Many years ago my husband was building a ferro-cement boat and decided to give up working in order to spend more time on it. I was supporting him while he did this. It became a problem for me when he did not spend nearly as much time on it as I thought he could have. I became very resentful but did not say anything about how I felt. Instead, I bought new clothes at every opportunity – I was constantly coming home with bags of new things. It was my passive-aggressive way of getting back at him. I was not dealing with the problem at all, I was just venting my resentment in a way which was not constructive.

Passive-aggression can be avoided through direct expression of your feelings and by telling people what you are and are not prepared to accept from them or to do for them. As I said earlier, I think it is perhaps the most destructive type of behaviour because it is distorted and difficult to deal with. It tends to undermine and destroy relationships.

BEHAVIOUR PATTERNS IN ACTION

I will give you an example of a situation I was involved in to illustrate further how the different types of behaviour work. I was parking my car one evening, misjudged backing into the space and hit the car behind me. The owner of the car happened to be sitting in the car, got out, came over, and in a sarcastic tone of voice said, 'You really should learn to stop before you hit other people's cars'. He was being aggressive. The process he would have gone through would run something like this:

Event – Woman backs into his car
Blame/Anger – 'It's her fault. Typical stupid woman driver. She shouldn't be allowed on the road.' Anger increases with self-inflammatory messages.
Frustration – 'It is her fault I am feeling angry. I have every right to be angry.' Feels righteous indignation.
Aggressive behaviour – 'You really should learn to stop before you hit other people's cars!'

For my part, I then had a choice as to how I reacted – aggressively, non-assertively, passive-aggressively, assertively:

AGGRESSIVE
Event – Man is aggressive towards me because I hit his car.
Blame/Anger – 'Creep! How dare he speak to me like that. Who does he think he is?' (Self-messages increase anger.)
Frustration – 'It's his fault I feel upset and angry. I'll show him.'
Aggressive behaviour – 'Don't you speak to me like that. Haven't you ever had an accident?'

NON-ASSERTIVE
Event – Man is aggressive towards me because I hit his car.
Blame/self-conscious, embarrassed – 'Oh dear I've done it again. I'm so stupid. I'm always doing the wrong thing.' (Self-messages create feelings of self-consciousness and embarrassment.)
Low self-esteem – The only place for self-esteem to go

is down.
Non-assertive behaviour – 'I'm terribly sorry. I'm always so hopeless at parking. Oh dear, so sorry.' (Being overly apologetic.)

PASSIVE-AGGRESSION
Event – Man is aggressive towards me because I hit his car.
Blame/Anger – 'Creep! How dare he speak to me like that. Who does he think he is?' (Self-messages increase anger.)
Frustration – 'It's his fault I feel upset and angry. I'll show him.'
Apparent non-assertive behaviour – 'I'm so terribly sorry. I'm so hopeless at parking.'
Passive-aggression – 'Of course, you men are so good at driving. You probably never have accidents.' (Delivered with an innocent expression. Leaves man with uncomfortable feeling that he is being 'got at', but he finds this hard to confront because it is unclear.)

ASSERTION
Event – Man is aggressive towards me because I hit his car.
No blame/responsibility – He is obviously very angry with me for hitting his car.
Constructive concern – I wonder how bad the damage is.
Positive feelings – Feel okay about self and other person. Concentrating on problem, not personalities.
Assertive behaviour – 'I'm sorry I hit your car. Would you like me to look at the damage.' (Spoken in calm but firm tone with direct eye contact and erect body posture.)

In this situation I did, in fact, respond assertively. The reason I was able to do so was because I accept that it is okay for me to make mistakes. Making mistakes is part of the human condition – none of us are perfect. I can learn from my mistakes and try to do better in the future. It is unnecessary and detrimental to me to give myself a hard time when I make a mistake. If you are able to accept that it is okay for you to make mistakes, you will often find yourself able to behave assertively when you have done so. Also, accepting that it is okay to make mistakes, has the effect of making you more tolerant of other people's mistakes.

The above example is a clear way of showing the process that leads to each type of behaviour and you will probably recognize yourself in all of them to a certain degree. You may also be thinking, 'It is not that simple' and, of course, you are right. Human beings are complex creatures and certainly cannot be fitted into a neat little chart so easily. Very often we will swing through one or more of the processes in a single situation. I might start out thinking, 'He's rotten to have done that'; move on to thinking, 'No, perhaps if I hadn't said this he would not have said that', and eventually I may focus on the situation and think about how I might deal with it by not blaming anyone. I have certainly been through more than one mode of behaviour on many occasions. However, bearing our human complexity in mind, the example given is still a most useful way of looking at what happens to lead us to behave in certain ways. It is only by raising your awareness of your behaviour and what leads to it that you can start to make changes.

4.
BODY
LANGUAGE

I have read differing opinions on how much of a message is verbal and how much is attributed to non-verbal aspects. However, despite the different opinions, you can accept that between 70 and 90 per cent of your communication messages are conveyed through non-verbal aspects. The verbal aspect means only the words, not the way they are said. The non-verbal aspect includes such things as:

- tone of voice
- inflection
- speed of speech
- eye contact
- body posture
- hand gestures
- facial expressions

For this reason, if you wish to become an effective communicator, it is important to have some knowledge and awareness of body language. With this knowledge and awareness, you will be able to look at your own behaviour and perhaps discover some of the reasons why you are not as effective as you would like to be in communicating with others. It can also be very useful to be able to pick up other people's non-verbal cues and tell whether they wish to receive your message in the way it is being sent – or at all. Sometimes people just do not want to hear what we are saying.

One of the problems is that we often send *mixed*

messages when we are communicating with others. We send mixed messages when we say one thing with our words and something else with our body. It then becomes confusing for the other person because they are getting two different messages. Since the body is far harder to fake than the words, they are more likely to believe the body. For example, imagine you are talking with someone and in words they say, 'Yes, what you are saying is most interesting. I would like to hear more about it.' At the same time they do not maintain eye contact with you and they occasionally look at their watch. Would you believe the words or the body?

In reading body language it is important to be aware that it is ambiguous – it can be interpreted incorrectly. In the above example you may come to the conclusion that the person is lying and they are not the least bit interested in what you are saying. The real issue may be that they are running over the time they had allotted to spend with you, they are expecting someone else to arrive at any moment and keep looking for them and are checking their watch to see how the time is going. They may well mean exactly what they are saying about being interested in what you have to say. Effective communication in this example would be to tell the truth – 'I am interested in what you have to say and want to hear more about it. However, I am expecting my next appointment to walk in at any minute and am unable to give you my full attention at this time. Perhaps we could arrange another meeting'. Here words and body are congruent, the message is clear, and there is little room for misinterpretation.

On the receiving end of a mixed message, it can be useful to check it out with the person. You could say, 'You say you are interested in what I have to say but you also seem distracted and I do not feel I have your full attention. Is there some problem?' Unfortunately, we live in a society where most people are very poor communicators.

As we become more skilled ourselves we can draw

people out and help them communicate more openly and honestly as illustrated above. There is a good reason why most people are poor communicators. It is something most of us have never been taught – I certainly never took a class in communication skills when I was at school. It is something that is supposed to come 'naturally' and which we 'pick up' from significant people in our lives like parents, relatives, teachers and friends. Unfortunately, they were never taught either, so they pass on forms of communication which are ineffective and sometimes destructive.

Assertion, aggression and non-assertion, being types of communication, have their own non-verbal components. Listed below are non-verbal features of each behaviour:

ASSERTIVE
Comfortably direct eye contact
Open body
Body tends to be still and relaxed
Posture upright
Shoulders straight
Voice appropriately firm/warm
Appropriate distance from other
Hand gestures emphasize words

AGGRESSIVE
Direct eye contact which becomes a battle
Looking bored
Pounding fist
Pointing finger
Hands on hips
Sarcastic tone
Loud voice
Deathly soft voice
Often invades other person's personal space
    by standing too close
Body closed off

NON-ASSERTIVE
Looking away
Smiling inappropriately
Fiddling with jewellery
Playing with hair
Wringing hands
Shuffling feet
Shoulders slumped
Voice soft and difficult to hear
Whining voice

What often happens when we are communicating is that we mix up body language across the three different types of behaviour. For example, I may be sending what I think is an assertive message and be using the right words, but I may be using body language which causes the message to be mixed:

Words – I would rather you did not leave the lid off the toothpaste. (*ASSERTIVE*)
Body language – Glaring eyes/Hands on hips. (*AGGRESSIVE*)
OR
Looking away/Smiling/Fiddling with jewellery. (*NON-ASSERTIVE*)

I said in the Introduction that this book is not intended as a substitute for an assertiveness training course. It is in the area of body language that working in a group can be particularly useful. Sometimes in roleplaying people will actually combine the body language of all three types of behaviour in one situation. At the end of the roleplay the roleplayer is given feedback from the teacher and the group and it shows them where they are being effective and where they are not being effective in communicating their message. It also helps the rest of the group to become aware of just how confusing and ineffective mixed messages are.

The first step in changing your behaviour is awareness. It is important to become aware of non-verbal behaviour and discover what you are doing that is preventing you from communicating effectively.

Start observing other people. I suggest starting with others because in non-verbal behaviour it is more difficult to observe yourself. Watch someone who you think is an effective communicator and see how they do it. What is it about their non-verbal behaviour that makes them effective? Also watch people who you think are ineffective and see what category they fit into and how they could change what they are doing to improve the communication. Please note that I am not suggesting you then tell them what they are doing wrong – it is rarely appreciated! The purpose is solely to raise your own awareness – and then transfer it to yourself.

Look at what you are doing. Do you maintain comfortably direct eye contact when talking to others or do you have difficulty doing so? How do you accentuate a point you want to make in a discussion – do you point your finger at the other person? When you want to be emotionally honest with someone, do you convey this through open body posture, or do you shut your body off with folded arms? What can you change in yourself? What do you *want* to change in yourself?

You may find that as you discover things you do not like in your behaviour, you seem to be doing them more often. I remember that when I 'discovered' body language, I decided I wanted to be more open and stop folding my arms across my chest. Once I had raised my awareness about it, I seemed to be doing it all the time. 'I'm getting worse', I thought. I was not actually getting worse – what was happening was that I was becoming more aware of my actions. This meant that I noticed what I was doing more often – so it appeared that I was getting worse. I did not find it easy to change this aspect of my body language, but it gradually became more natural to me and now I feel quite uncomfortable with my arms crossed – unless it is cold!

Now I have talked about body language and the part it plays in assertion, I shall move onto the very important verbal skill of communicating feelings.

5.
'I' MESSAGES

'I' messages play a large part in assertive behaviour. They include messages about feelings, thoughts, beliefs and values – I feel, I think, I believe, I value. In this chapter I will be focusing on 'I' messages for communicating feelings. The reason for focusing particularly on feelings is that most people have difficulty in expressing their feelings openly and honestly. In themselves, feelings are not a problem, but most of us have difficulty in expressing them in a way which is constructive and opens up communication. We often express them in ways which are unclear and which can be experienced as an attack by the other person. If you attack someone, be it physical or verbal, they are likely to either fight back or to withdraw. Communication becomes either destructive or non-existent. 'I' messages are an effective way of communicating feelings to others.

Most of us have learned to communicate feelings in the form of 'You' messages. The chart on page 46 shows the same message being communicated in the form of both a 'You' message and an 'I' message. You will see that the two different forms of communication, in fact, make the messages quite different.

The example given in the chart shows the communication of a negative feeling. 'I' messages are not only concerned with negatives, they are also used to communicate positive feelings:

'I feel very happy when you send me flowers.'
instead of
'You make me very happy when you're so thoughtful.'

'YOU' MESSAGE	'I' MESSAGE
You (**Disowning**) make me feel angry (**Blame**) when you're so unreliable (**Judgement of behaviour**).	I (**Owning**) feel angry (**Communication of feeling**) when you arrive late (**Description of behaviour**).
Disowning When I say 'You' in communicating a feeling, I disown it. I do not take any responsibility for it. It is not my problem, it is yours.	**Owning** When I say 'I' in communicating a feeling, I own it. I take responsibility for it. It is my problem.
Blame When I say 'You make me feel angry'. I blame you for the way I feel and make you responsible for it. After all, if you had not been so unreliable I would not be feeling the way I am. In using a 'You' message I am seeking to change you so I do not have to feel angry anymore. I am making my anger your problem.	**Communication of feeling** When I say 'I feel angry', I take responsibility for the way I feel. My feeling of anger is my particular reaction to your late arrival. Someone else might have a different response, but 'I feel angry'. In using an 'I' message I am communicating to you the way I feel without making it your problem.
Judgement of behaviour In saying 'when you're so unreliable' I am passing a judgement upon your behaviour. I have made the judgement: arriving late = being unreliable	**Description of behaviour** In saying 'when you arrive late' I am merely describing the behaviour which I feel angry about. I have made no judgement about what being late means.

Being responsible for another person's happiness can be as heavy a burden to carry as being responsible for their unhappiness. It is the other side of the same coin – 'You make me happy when you do the things I like' ... *and* ... 'You make me unhappy when you do the things I don't like'. Both are saying, 'You are responsible for me!'

Apart from the important *responsibility* aspect of 'I' messages, they are also extremely clear communication messages. I tell you what I feel – and I tell you the exact behaviour that I have the feeling about. There is no room whatsoever for misinterpretation. Evaluative words such as:

- unreliable
- irresponsible
- inconsiderate

- kind
- generous
- considerate
- immature
- selfish
- mature
- unselfish

are unclear in their meaning. All these words involve a 'value judgement' and these are always subjective. What I would classify as 'selfish' may not be what you would classify as selfish. What you consider to be 'immature' behaviour may not be immature in my eyes. Both are based on subjective judgements on my part about what does or does not constitute selfish or immature behaviour. (You will find further discussion of the role of Values in communication in Chapter 7).

'I' messages are an extremely effective form of communication message and this is due to a number of factors:

- Responsibility lies with the sender of the message. I own my feelings – I do not 'dump' them onto you. If I feel angry I may want to tell you about it, but the anger is *my* problem.

- When we feel attacked by others we have a natural desire to defend ourselves or attack back. Since an 'I' message is not an attack on the other person, their need to defend themselves or attack back is greatly diminished. This means that open communication is more likely to take place.

- Describing the other person's behaviour gives them feedback without judgement or evaluation of what they have done. We all need to give and receive feedback. If I do not tell you that I feel angry when you arrive late, how are you to know? If you do not tell me that you feel hurt when I spend more time with other friends than with you, how am I going to know?

I have personally found 'I' messages to be extremely useful in my relationships with other people. Communication is a two-way process and this type of message is an open invitation to the other person to engage themselves in communication. There is no guarantee that they will take up the invitation – other people do not always want to communicate with us. If this is so, then I would consider it was no longer my problem. I have been open and honest with you about my feelings and given you a clear message about the behaviour involved – should you refuse to communicate with me, as is your right, I need to look for other ways of dealing with the situation and my feelings about it. You may decide that you will accept the invitation to communicate and after having done so, refuse to meet my needs. Again, this is your right, and I need to look for other ways to deal with the situation and my feelings.

'I' messages require courage. When you express yourself through this type of message you expose yourself and it can leave you feeling vulnerable. 'You' messages concentrate on the other person while 'I' messages concentrate on me. For example, I have been to a party and the man I was with spent most of the evening talking to other women. I could confront him with a 'You' message – 'You are really ill-mannered at parties and if you think I am going to put up with that sort of behaviour you are mistaken.' This focuses entirely on the other person, says nothing about me and tends to close down communication. Alternatively, I could use an 'I' message – 'I felt hurt and insecure when you spent most of the evening with other women.' This focuses on my feelings, makes no evaluation of the other person and tends to open up communication. I am sure you will see that in the 'I' message I am likely to feel vulnerable because I have exposed myself. It can be extremely frightening to do so. Authentic relationships require risk-taking or they never become real. If I want to relate to you in an authentic way and create intimacy in the relationship, then I must be prepared to expose myself. Try it – you might just find that you have some very rewarding results.

6.
COMPLIMENTS ARE GIFTS

I think of compliments as gifts because they are something positive which I can give to others or receive from them. The trouble is that they are often given or received in ways which can diminish or even annihilate them. We can turn a positive into a negative. There are a number of ways in which people deal with compliments which are not particularly useful. You may well recognize yourself in some of the responses:

Sender – I think you are very attractive.
Receiver – Who me? You're just saying that. (Shyly looks away, giggles and fiddles with hair)
   The person receiving the compliment has communicated that they do not feel they deserve it. The receiver communicates non-acceptance.

Sender – I think you have a wonderful body.
Receiver – I bet you say that to all the men.
   By joking the receiver has communicated non-acceptance of the compliment.

Sender – I like your shirt.
Receiver – I like yours too.
   The receiver has shifted the attention away from him/herself and not accepted the compliment.

Sender – I like your dress.
Receiver – What this old rag. I've had it for years and it was really cheap.
   Here the receiver has destroyed the compliment by

communicating, 'No thanks, I don't want it'.

An assertive response to a compliment is simply to receive it:

Sender – I think you've written a good report.
Receiver – Thank you.
A person has given you a gift and it is received.

You can also go a step further in the acceptance of a compliment and acknowledge or affirm yourself:

Sender – I think you've written a good report.
Receiver – Thank you. I'm really pleased with it too.
The gift is received and the receiver also adds to the power of the gift by agreeing with it.

There are also negative ways of giving compliments to others:

Sender – This cake is delicious. I wish I were a good cook like you.
Here the sender puts him/herself down while building the other person up. It is not necessary to make any comparisons about yourself or your abilities when paying compliments.

Sender – Of course, you are so intelligent you have the answer to everything.
It could be disputed whether this is a compliment at all. It would be most uncomfortable to be on the receiving end of this one.

Sender – I think your eyes would look even more beautiful if you were lying on a green pillow.
This compliment involves sexual innuendo – I think you have beautiful eyes and I would like to go to bed with you. Many people feel ill at ease when given this type of compliment.

Sender – I think you're very attractive. I can't understand why nobody else does.

This compliment was related to me by someone who had received it 30 years earlier. It is fairly obvious why she had not forgotten it!

An assertive way of giving a compliment is simple, direct and clear:

Sender – I think you are a good cook.
I think you are very intelligent.
I think you have beautiful eyes.
I find you very attractive.

In all of the above the message is simple, to the point, and leaves no room for misinterpretation. You will also notice that they are spoken in 'I' messages – the sender takes responsibility for their own opinion. Sometimes people give compliments as if they were objective facts:

Sender – You are so beautiful.

Who says so? The sender removes him/herself from the message – they disown it. Beauty is in the eye of the beholder – I might think you are beautiful, but it is not necessarily the case that everyone does.

In the giving of compliments, as in all aspects of assertion, it is important to take responsibility for your own opinions. I also find it aggravating when people speak for me when giving a compliment. For example, a flatmate and I have had a friend staying with us for the weekend and as the friend was leaving, my flatmate said, 'We really enjoyed having you to stay with us'. In saying 'we' my flatmate has spoken for me. Maybe I did enjoy it, but maybe I did not. Whatever is the case, I am quite capable of speaking for myself if I choose to.

Self-esteem plays a large part in my ability to both give and receive compliments. If I do not feel very good about myself in a particular area, then it will be difficult for me to accept a compliment about it. For example, a friend paid me a compliment not so long ago about my hands. He said, 'I think you have nice hands.' I said, 'Thank you.' I know the rules about receiving compliments assertively, but inside I was busy annihilating the compliment by saying things to myself like, 'He can't really mean that. My fingers are short and stubby and my nails are not very long.' Many times we will appear to accept compliments, but be busy destroying them in our minds. However, even this need not be disastrous because the person's message can start to filter through and help to change your perception of yourself. The reason I have used this particular example is because I was looking at my hands this morning and I thought, 'They do look rather nice. I think I am getting to like them'. My friend's compliment helped me to change my perception of myself.

Many of us feel that our perception of ourselves is the correct one. After all I am the only one who really knows me, therefore, my perception is right and yours is wrong! I would argue that it is very useful for us to listen to other people's perceptions of us and not to disregard them too easily. They can be very useful to us in changing the way we see ourselves to a more positive way. It was through other people's perceptions of me that I was able to make a major change in my life.

I left school at the age of fifteen having hated it while I was there. My parents allowed me to leave then because my rebellious behaviour was leading me towards expulsion. In fact, the Reverend Mother would have already expelled me if she had had her way! I then went into a government department where I learned to type and stayed there for almost two years working in a typing pool. From there, I worked in various office and secretarial jobs until 1981 when at the age of 36 I went to university full-time. I had then been working as a secretary for 20 years.

I had held the very strong belief that I was unintelligent. I covered it up with a certain bravado – 'I could have done it if I had wanted to and had not hated school so much' – but inside I felt I was inadequate in this area. A few years before I returned to study people started paying me compliments about my intelligence – 'You are very bright. Have you thought about studying or doing something different?' At first I did not believe them – and thought they were mistaken in their observation. I was fortunate in getting quite a number of these types of compliments and gradually I started to think that maybe there was some truth in what they were saying.

With trepidation I enrolled at a technical college. I was so unsure of myself that my first essay, consisting of one foolscap page, took me three hours to write! The teachers were wonderful – full of compliments and positive feedback. They were well aware that the major problem confronting mature students is lack of confidence. I got through that year with lots of compliments and encouragement, passed the exams and was accepted into university. I completed a Bachelor of Arts degree in 1983, with very good grades.

Today I believe I am an intelligent person, but I do not think it really filtered through until a couple of years ago. It was a long, slow, gradual process because my belief that I was unintelligent was so deep and strong. Even when I got 'A' grades at university, I would think to myself, 'Maybe it was just a fluke', or 'Perhaps it is just because the lecturer likes me'. I found it very difficult to take credit and accept that I was both capable and intelligent.

Through those first compliments, my life has changed. From doing work that I found unchallenging and boring, I am now a teacher doing something that I consider to be worthwhile and making a contribution to society by helping people to develop their full potential. Compliments are powerful things – *if you let them in!*

I hope that the next time you receive a compliment you will think about what it can do for your self-esteem and your perception of yourself. Bear in mind that most of us have problems with self-esteem – *open up, accept them, change yourself!*

7.
VALUES

Values can create problems in acting assertively and it is useful to understand something about them and to recognize when values are the issue at stake in a conflict situation. The reason why values are problematic is that we tend to feel very strongly about them, and not only feel strongly, but feel that we are *right*. My values are right – your values are wrong. This sort of position is troublesome to assertion because it sets up a win/lose situation:

I am right . . . You are wrong
I must win . . . You must lose

This is not assertive nor is it conducive to open communication. Communication is a two-way process – I express myself/You express yourself. There is no communication unless real listening occurs. This means to be open to the other person, to understand what they are saying, to try and put yourself in their position and *hear* them. There is a big difference between what passes for listening – and hearing what someone is saying. Carl Rogers, the well-known psychotherapist, claims that our inability to listen properly is the greatest barrier to interpersonal communication there is.

Under certain circumstances you may not care whether you are really communicating or not. You may feel so strongly about something that you are not concerned about the state of your relationship with the other person. I have felt like this myself. The important thing to be aware of is that relationships are damaged by railroading and bullying people. They may do what you want, they may even pay lip-service by telling you that you are right, but the price you may have to pay for getting your own way and proving your point may be very high indeed. You will see relationships where one person is the bully and imposes their opinions and values on the other. The other may go along with them for the sake of peace, but you will probably also find them undermining their partner in subtle ways. Bullying creates resentment and resentment will come out in some way. If you value your relationships it is worth thinking about this.

There is nothing wrong with having values – in themselves they are not a problem. It is what we do with them when we come into conflict that is the problem. They present themselves constantly and do not just involve such lofty things as freedom, equality, justice, etc. They also represent such mundane matters as whether you like the lid left on or off the toothpaste, whether you prefer to live in a tidy or untidy house, whether you prefer your friends to be punctual or do not mind if they are late. Values are something which come up constantly in our everyday lives and can cause us great discomfort.

I really became aware of the problem of values when I was at university. I studied philosophy and within that discipline I took some courses in moral philosophy. In one particular course, we looked at topics that often cause conflict such as euthanasia, vivisection and abortion. I chose to do one of my assignments on abortion because it was a moral issue that I could find no clear answer to. I had heard emotional arguments from both sides and could feel sympathy for both. 'At last', I thought, 'an opportunity to come to an objective decision about this moral issue.' But at the end of the assignment I had no clear answers and even today I still hope it is something I shall never have to make a decision about. The reason I remain unclear is that for every good argument on one side (and I am talking about so-called objective, logical arguments, not emotive ones), there is an equally good argument on the other side.

My purpose in telling you this is to point out that if someone were to ask you to support *objectively* the reasons why you prefer people to be punctual you may find there are some good reasons on the other side too. You will only be able to *hear* the good reasons if you are prepared to listen. If you enter the discussion believing yourself to be right and the other person to be wrong you will not be listening and you will not be focusing on the problem.

One of the conflicts of value I have had over and over again for years is the value of tidiness. I prefer to live in a tidy environment, but I have shared living accommodation with a number of people for whom tidiness is not a high priority. Please note my language in expressing this because language plays such a large part in determining feeling and attitudes. Once I would have expressed this by saying, 'I prefer to live in a clean and tidy house, but have shared with a string of messy people'. This form of expression is laden with judgement and emotion in my reference to 'messy' people. I have one of my most difficult living situations to thank for a new awareness about language and values.

I was sharing a home with a woman whom I shall call Carol. When I first started sharing with her I would have called her messy, untidy, selfish and inconsiderate. I felt very self-righteous in my neatness and organization, and very angry that she did not do her share of the cleaning. One of the times I confronted her about it I did so in this way – 'I am fed up with you leaving dishes in the sink and leaving me to clean up the mess'. She said very little at the time as she was quite taken aback by my onslaught. She was away for a few days and when she returned she told me she had felt extremely angry at the way I had approached her and that I needed to understand that cleaning and tidying was not 'high on her list of priorities'. It was this last comment that really made me think. Until then I had honestly thought that people who were untidy were somehow inadequate and had a definite 'flaw' in their characters. From Carol's comment I realized that it was just that she held different values to me.

I made a number of mistakes in the way I handled this situation:

- I confronted the situation believing I was *right* and with the attitude that she was wrong and inadequate and if she would only smarten up then everything would be fine.

- Although I used an 'I' message, I took it too far. It was not necesary for me to add 'leaving me to clear up the mess'. In fact she said, 'I never expected you to clean up the mess'. By accusing her of expecting me to do it, I attributed her with motives that were perhaps not there.

- I did not open up a conversation to discuss the issue. I had felt quite nervous about saying anything to her and had just 'flung' the words out in a rush – she felt attacked and was unable to respond at the time. When she did respond she was, in fact, far more calm and assertive than I had been. She taught me a great deal.

- My belief in my *rightness* was a major problem in the way I handled this situation. If I had approached it with an awareness that we had a conflict of values which we needed to sort out and with the view that neither her nor my values were right (just *different*) then we may have been able to deal with the conflict more effectively.

The following is the kind of approach that would have been conducive to open communication:

Beverley – Carol, I would like to talk to you about something. Do you have time now?
Carol – No, I am just off to work. I will be home at 7.00 pm, perhaps we could discuss it then.

Beverley – Yes, fine.

Later

Beverley – I am feeling a bit upset about the cleaning and tidying up situation in the house. I feel I am doing more than my fair share and would like to talk about this.

Carol – Well, the problem is that I obviously prefer to live in a more casual environment than you do. A bit of untidiness does not bother me. I would rather put my energy into doing other things.

Beverley – I can understand that it is not important to you, but we are sharing together and both need to feel comfortable here. Do you have any suggestions as to how we could both compromise a little and try to meet each other's needs.

Carol – Yes, I guess I could try to be a bit tidier in the living areas, and perhaps you could be tolerant if I forget sometimes and leave things around.

Beverley – Yes, let's give this a try and if it doesn't work we can talk about it again.

In the above conversation, communication was opened up and a solution was reached. It is quite possible that the solution reached might not work. In that event it would need to be discussed again. If the situation became intolerable for either party, perhaps we would have to decide that we were too incompatible to live together.

Just as you and I have the right to our own feelings, thoughts and beliefs, we also have the right to hold our own values. We have the right to hold them – but that does not make them *right*!

8.
MAKING AND REFUSING REQUESTS

One of the major reasons people state for coming to an assertiveness training class is to learn to say 'No' – such a small word and yet one that for many is very difficult to say. They often go further than this and say, 'I would like to learn to say no without feeling guilty'. There are no guarantees that you will not feel guilty as you change your behaviour. I certainly had to come to terms with guilt feelings as I became more assertive. However, although I do sometimes still experience guilt when I take a new step with assertion, there are numerous situations which do not bring up the slightest feeling of guilt – and I am talking about situations which I would once have agonized over. You may find that you do not say no to people because you do not want to experience guilt. It is a very unpleasant emotion to feel and you may think it is not worth it. I would suggest that it is worth experiencing it because it will dissipate as you start believing that you have the right to say no.

If you decide you will continue to be non-assertive to avoid guilt feelings, the following repeating process is likely to occur:

NON-ASSERTION . . . LOW SELF-ESTEEM . . .
NON-ASSERTION . . . LOWER SELF-ESTEEM etc.

Your self-esteem will suffer from continued non-assertion. If, on the other hand, you decide to experience your guilt, the following process is likely to occur:

ASSERTION ... GUILT ... ASSERTION ... LESS GUILT ... ASSERTION ... EVEN LESS GUILT ... EVENTUALLY – NO GUILT

As you allow yourself to experience guilt and start to question its validity, you will find that it dissipates and eventually you will no longer experience it. What you will find in this chapter are some of the beliefs which underlie the inability to say no when you want to. Awareness of these beliefs will enable you to challenge and change them.

WON'T VS CAN'T

Once again I want to look at the responsibility aspect in refusing requests. Very often, instead of a direct, honest 'No', we offer excuses for why we 'can't' do something. I want to look at the word 'can't' and the implications it has in terms of taking responsibility for our actions and decisions. How often do you find yourself saying things like 'I can't come out tonight because I have to wash my hair' or 'I can't take the rubbish out right now because I am in the middle of watching a television programme'. The question to ask yourself when you find yourself saying 'I can't' is 'Is this a statement of something that is impossible?'. 'Can't' seems to imply being unable, crippled or controlled from the outside. If it is not impossible then you would be taking responsibility if you substituted such words as 'I won't', 'I don't want to', 'I would rather not' or 'I would prefer not to'. Take the first example – 'I can't come out tonight because I have to wash my hair'. Is it really impossible? Do you *have to* wash your hair? Or is it that you have made a decision that tonight you *want* to wash your hair. An assertive refusal would be 'I *would rather not* come out tonight because I *want* to wash my hair'. Similarly, the second example can be easily changed to an assertive statement – 'I *do not want* to take the rubbish out right now because I am in the middle of watching a television programme'. In these examples responsibility is taken for the person's decision to refuse the request. The statement is stronger and is more likely to be taken seriously.

I will give you a personal example where I took no responsibility for a decision I had made. A woman friend phoned me and asked me if I would go out to dinner the following Friday. I refused by saying, 'No, I would rather not because I usually see David on Friday nights' (assertive refusal). She then explained that it was her birthday and she was arranging dinner with a few friends. I then said, 'In that case I would like to come' (an assertive acceptance since it was true). Up until then I had been assertive. When David rang and suggested we see each other on Friday night I said, 'I *can't* because I *have to* go to a birthday dinner'. My statement was a complete denial of responsibility for my decision to go to the dinner. I also played 'victim' – poor me, I have to go! It was untrue that I could not go out with him. Of course I could have if I had wanted to. By saying 'I have to' I was saying I had no choice in the matter – of course I had a choice, no-one was holding a gun at my head. An assertive response to his request would have been 'No, I won't come out this Friday because it is a friend's birthday and I want to help her celebrate'. And to alleviate the possibility of him feeling rejected I could have said, 'I do want to see you, could we make it another night?' Being assertive can include being concerned about the other person's feelings – it does not need to be abrasive.

I would like to talk a little further about 'can't' and 'won't' and how the refusal to take responsibility disempowers you. People often say things like 'I can't lose weight', 'I can't stop smoking' or 'I can't get up in the morning' and innumerable other such statements.

You disempower yourself with these types of statements for two reasons:

- By constantly saying you can't do something, you reinforce a negative belief – it becomes a self-fulfilling prophecy. Can you imagine if a team of footballers told themselves over and over again that they could not win. What do you think their chances of winning would be?
- You invest something outside of yourself with tremendous power – food controls me; cigarettes control me; my bed controls me.

You will find yourself greatly empowered when you take responsibility. It is far easier to move from:

$$I won't. \rightarrow I will.$$
than from:
$$I can't. \rightarrow I will.$$

One of the things I used to say was 'I can't stop smoking'. Instead of taking responsibility and accepting that I enjoyed smoking and did not want to stop, I gave cigarettes power over me. I eventually accepted responsibility and spent some time saying 'I won't stop smoking'. When I was ready I did stop. I moved from:

$$I can't \rightarrow \quad I won't \quad \rightarrow I will$$
$$\text{(Victim) \quad (Responsibility) \quad (Action)}$$

BELIEFS AND REFUSING REQUESTS

Beliefs underlie our behaviour. If I can look at my beliefs and change them, then the way in which I relate to others will change. Assertion is not merely a matter of learning skills – that part is superficial and ineffective unless the underlying beliefs are also changed. Underneath the inability to say no will be beliefs about what saying no means. I will go through some of the thoughts that can be a problem in refusing requests.

I can't say no, they will be terribly disappointed.
In many situations it is useful to be able to differentiate whose problem it is. In the above situation you might ask yourself 'If a person reacts with disappointment to my refusal, whose problem is it?'. Suppose your friend is disappointed – that is fair enough, he/she has a right to be disappointed. But their disappointment is their problem, not yours. If you make it yours by feeling really bad about it, then it will be difficult to refuse. It is a fact of life that sometimes we face disappointments – it is something we need to come to terms with. I would like to point out that working out whose problem it is does not mean having an uncaring attitude. I can say to myself that your disappointment is your problem and not be immobilized or manipulated by it, whilst at the same time feeling *appropriate* concern for you. For example:

Jane – Would you like to go to a film tonight?
John – No, I would rather not. I want to stay in and have a quiet night.
Jane – Oh, I really had hoped you would come. There isn't anyone else I can ask. (disappointment)
John – I understand you may feel disappointed and I'm sorry about that, but I am looking forward to a night at home, so it is no this time.

Here the refusal has been direct and honest, and concern has been appropriate. John has accepted Jane's right to feel disappointed and expressed concern for her, but he has also let it be her problem. He is not going to ruin his evening at home feeling guilty for refusing – nor is he going to forego his desire for that night at home in order to do something he does not want to do.

I can't say no, they will be so hurt.

What if your friend is hurt? There is no difference
between this and the last situation. Remember that we
choose our own emotions and if your friend feels hurt,
that is their problem. They have every right to express
their hurt (in a non-blaming way) and you may wish to
express your concern – and still do what you want.
Hurt, over-sensitivity or weakness can be used as a
manipulative tool. If I present the image that I am
very easily hurt and do not handle disappointments
very well, I can manipulate you into doing what I
want. Weakness can be very powerfully used. In
playing along with a person who behaves in this way,
you do not help them to develop into a stronger person,
you assist them in staying just the way they are.
Again, there is no need to be uncaring in your refusal
– just firm!

They may not like me anymore.

Let us look at the reality of this belief. I would say it is
possible that the person may not like you anymore!
The question that then arises is 'If this relationship is
dependent upon my always meeting the other person's
needs, then how good a relationship is it?'. Do I want a
relationship that is so unequal, one where I must
squash my needs and desires and always meet the
other person's? It may be difficult to face and accept
that some of your relationships actually survive on this
basis. If the relationship feels so important that you
are not prepared to risk it, then do not assert yourself.
On the other hand, it is possible that if you are
prepared to take the risk, you may find that the person
does still like you. They may be taken aback when you
change your behaviour – that is quite understandable –
but you may find that they not only still like you, they
also have greater respect for you.

It must be important or they would not have asked.

Again, let us look at the reality of this statement.

People are different – they do not all feel the same about the same things. Because you would only ask if it were important does not mean others feel the same – they may, but it is just as likely they may not. Ask yourself 'How important are my own needs? Is this friend's need more important than my own?'. Say your friend asks you to get him or her a book during your lunch hour and you had planned to go for a swim. Is his or her need for the book more important than your need to have a swim? Very often we push our own needs aside and treat other's as more important.

They may prefer you to say no if you don't want to do something.
Then there is the person who does not mind if you say no to things you do not want to do and who prefers you to speak the truth so they know where they stand with you. They may be disappointed, but they accept disappointment as a reality of life and are not immobilized by it. They are probably also quite comfortable saying no themselves.

NEEDS – YOURS AND MINE

Relationships involve fulfilling each other's needs – mutual give and take. Remember that you owe it to yourself to meet your own needs as well. The person with healthy self-esteem looks after themselves as well as other people. One of the things I discovered when I started teaching was that I was getting tired very quickly and was starting to suffer from 'burn out' – a trap which people in the helping professions can easily fall into. The problem was that I was not taking care of myself – I was not setting high enough limits on how much I was prepared to give to my students. What I also discovered was that as I became more tired, I also became less effective in my teaching. By not taking care of myself, I was doing my students a disservice. I am now able to set limits – to say no when I want to. I take better care of myself and my teaching is more effective. I will not be able to nurture and support you unless I also nurture and support me. Become more aware of the thoughts that go through your mind when you want to say no and look at them realistically. (Chapter 11 on self-talk will give you some hints on how to do this).

After I did my first assertion course, I found that when people made requests of me I still tended to say yes. I was so used to saying yes that it had become a habit for me. I would then go away and think 'I do not have to say yes all the time now, I have the right to say no!'. Then I would contact the other person involved and tell them I had changed my mind and did not want to do it after all. I found I had a number of angry people around me, because they felt they could not get a straight answer from me. Realizing that I was responding from habit and that on many occasions I really did not know whether I wanted to do something or not, I decided to give myself time to think. For a period of time in response to requests I would say 'I am not sure, I will think about it and let you know'. I found others reacted quite favourably to this response from me. I was so unused to considering my own needs that I really did not know what they were and what I did and did not want to do. By giving myself time to think I came to be more in touch with myself, my needs and my wants. I was then able to respond more quickly with a yes or no as the situation demanded. If you are like me in this respect, you may find it useful to use this delaying tactic. You do have the right to think before making a decision.

Another problem I experienced when I first started being assertive was that at times I was a bit abrasive in my refusal to do things I did not want to do. The reason for this was that I felt extremely uncomfortable and guilty saying no. Because I felt this way, my words would come out in a rush and seem quite abrupt. As I became more comfortable and my guilt started to disappear, my refusals became more relaxed and more caring. Do not expect too much from yourself –

sometimes you will make mistakes and sometimes you will feel miserable about the way you have handled a situation or at other times you will handle them very well. It is part of the process of learning something new. When you decided to learn to drive, I am sure you did not jump straight into the driver's seat and become an expert overnight. Learning to change behaviour is different to learning to drive only insofar as it is probably more difficult. In learning to drive you are trying to master something new – in changing behaviour you have to alter the old *in addition* to learning something new. Be kind to yourself. Treat yourself gently. Accept yourself when you make mistakes. Encourage yourself when you succeed. Learn to be your *own* best friend.

BELIEFS AND MAKING REQUESTS

How many of us ask for what we want from other people honestly and openly? I know I ask for much more from people than I used to, but there are still certain areas with which I have difficulty. As with the refusing of requests, there are underlying beliefs which create problems for us in making requests.

The other person may not be able to refuse.
This is one of the beliefs I still have difficulty with. I am aware that many people do not say no when they want to and I find it difficult to cope with the thought that they are doing something they do not want to do and, on many occasions, resenting me for it. Here is a prime example of getting caught up in the other person's problem. If a person is unable to say no to my request – it is their problem. If they resent me in doing something they do not want to do' – that is also their problem. I probably fear this one the most, because of the many times in the past when I have done things I did not want to do and resented the person who asked. I have also on occasions made it clear in passive-aggressive ways that I did not really want to be there.

For example, I have been out with someone I did not want to go out with and spent the evening behaving in a withdrawn and bored manner. When asked what was wrong I would say, 'Nothing, I am just a bit tired' or 'I have a headache'. I suspect many people have been on the receiving end of this type of behaviour at times in their lives. Rejection may hurt, but I think this type of reaction is far more hurtful and confusing. We do not say no because we do not want to hurt the other person, but we probably hurt them more and leave them feeling confused and angry.

The other person may say no.
We sometimes think like this – 'If I ask this person out and they refuse me, I will be rejected and that would be awful'. The problem many of us have is that we take things too far in our heads – refusal = rejection. It is not necessarily true that when a person says no to us they are rejecting us. They may have other plans or they may be involved in a committed relationship, etc. We are sometimes so expectant of rejection that we perceive the other person's response as rejection when it may not be. For example, a few years ago a man I had met at a party rang me and asked me out to dinner. My response was 'Just a minute I will check my diary'. As it happened I was not free that night and once I had said that he quickly terminated the call and did not call again. I heard later through a mutual acquaintance that he had said, 'She obviously did not want to go or she would not have had to look in her diary'. This was not true – I always check my diary before making arrangements. He perceived rejection where none was intended.

Why is it that most of us have such a problem with rejection? I would suggest that it is because we again take things too far – refusal = rejection = there is something wrong with me. A refusal from someone may, in fact, be rejection. Maybe they do not like me or maybe they do not find me attractive. Does that mean there is something wrong with me? Their rejection will tell us more about them than it will about me. For example, suppose I were to ask a man out to dinner and he refuses. What does it tell you about me? Nothing! It may tell us a number of things about him, such as:

- He prefers blondes to brunettes.
- He does not like going out to dinner.
- He likes blue eyes, not brown.
- He prefers women who wait for him to ask them out!

By the same token, if a man asks me out to a party and I refuse, it tells you nothing about him but it may tell you something about me:

- I like sensitive men.
- I like men who treat me as an equal.
- I don't like parties.
- I prefer going out to dinner.

His refusal does not mean there is anything wrong with me, nor does mine mean there is anything wrong with him. I am not his type – and he is not mine. End of story. If we all liked the same types we would really have problems!

Our minds are wonderful tools which we often use in ways which are detrimental to ourselves. For example, if I were to go into a shop and buy Cheddar cheese because I like its colouring and character, you would not find the Edam and Gorgonzola getting themselves into a frenzy wondering why they were not chosen and trying to change themselves so they were more marketable! It takes the human mind to get off onto those sorts of trips.

It is appropriate to feel hurt if you have been rejected. It is disappointing – it *does* hurt. Try not to take it further into picking yourself to pieces and giving yourself a hard time. That is self-destructive and counter-productive.

I will feel under an obligation to them.

When someone asks me to do something for them and I
agree, I think of what I am doing as a 'free' gift. I am
not doing it because I have an expectation of a return
favour – I am doing it because I want to. Now this is
not to say that there is not a relationship between
doing things for others and having them do things for
you. If a relationship is one-sided and one person
constantly gives and the other takes, then it is not a
very balanced or equal relationship. People are more
likely to treat doing you a favour as a 'free' gift, if they
feel there is the freedom to say no.

MANIPULATION AND GUILT TRIPS

People are more likely to be able to feel free to say no
if your requests of them are devoid of manipulation or
guilt trips. I will give you an example of a
manipulative, guilt-inducing request that was made of
me by an acquaintance I had been doing some work
with – 'Would you like to help a friend in need?'. The
implication in this request was being a friend =
helping/not helping = not being a friend. My reaction
to this request was irritation because I knew what was
happening. However, I was able to say no, because I
did not 'buy into' the inference that 'being a friend =
helping'. In my progress to becoming more assertive I
can see that I would have had different reactions at
different times. At one time I would have 'bought into'
the guilt trip – I would have accepted that 'being a
friend = helping'. Further along in my development I
would have realized I was being manipulated, been
furious with her for her 'awful' behaviour, said no, and
still have felt some guilt. I was still partly accepting
the premise 'being a friend = helping'. When it did
actually happen, I felt slight irritation, but I also felt
quite comfortable saying no. Because someone attempts
to manipulate me, I do not have to allow them to
succeed. I need to first take responsibility for the fact
that I can only be manipulated if I allow it to happen.

Once I take this responsibility it becomes easier to say no.

Often requests are made wanting the other person to say yes, and in wanting this we try to manipulate them into doing so. If you are able to make requests of others in a free way, willing to accept either a yes or a no, then it gives them more freedom to be honest about what they want to do. When this freedom enters into relationships they become more honest and authentic. We pay a price in resentment from the other when we manipulate them through guilt. They may do it but the price is very high!

In this chapter I have talked about the right to say no. In the following chapter I will discuss personal rights and the part they play in making someone more spontaneous and authentic.

9.
PERSONAL RIGHTS

Assertive philosophy is based on a belief that we all have personal rights. In each of the definitions of the three types of behaviour rights are mentioned:

Assertion – Expressing yourself in a way which does not violate other people's rights.
Non-assertion – Allowing others to violate your rights.
Aggression – Always violates the other person's rights.

What are personal rights? They are rights a person can take on that enable them to take assertive action. Their purpose is to help you change your beliefs about yourself – thus allowing you to relate to others and to the outside world in a different way. It should be noted that written into personal rights (and assertion as a whole) is the proviso that they do not violate other people's rights. For example, the right to kill is not an assertive personal right because it violates other people's rights. A contentious personal right which comes up often is 'the right to smoke'. Many non-smokers feel this violates their right to clean air. Some are much clearer than others. The purpose of taking on any right is that it enables you to take action you may not otherwise feel free to take.

I am going to give you some examples of personal rights that I have taken on and show you how they have made a difference to my life. You may relate closely to some of them while others may have very little meaning for you. I think the important thing is to construct your own list of rights – ones that have meaning for you and which you can apply to your own life.

THE RIGHT TO BE TREATED WITH RESPECT

I now believe that I have the right to be treated with respect. This does not mean that because I believe it, I always get it. Again, I have said that these rights are not concerned with changing the world, but rather with changing beliefs and relating to the world in a different way. Now that I believe I have this right, I approach everything I do in a different way to the time when I did not believe I had it. I walk into gatherings with upright body language – my body conveys the message, 'I expect to be respected'. Others may not be able to put it into words, but they receive the message.

There was a time when I felt extremely inferior to and intimidated by certain authority figures. At university I could hardly speak to lecturers because I thought they were so brilliant and I was so stupid. I certainly did not expect to be treated with respect. For the most part they were very kind people and did not take advantage of this by treating me as I believed I should be treated. However, to a large degree it prevented me from relating to them as equals – I was unable to develop the type of relationships with them that I would have liked. Now this is no longer a problem for me. I know there are many people who are better educated than me, who know things I do not know, who have skills I do not have – but on the level of being a human being that does not make them any better than me or more deserving of respect. The same applies in the other direction – I am better educated than some people, I know things that others do not, I have skills that others do not have – that does not make me better than they are. On the human level we are all equals. Now it does not matter to me whether someone is a rubbish collector or a lecturer, a housemaid or a psychiatrist – we are all equally deserving of respect.

As I said, because I believe I have the right to be treated with respect does not mean I always am. However, if someone treats me in a disrespectful way I am now able to deal with it effectively. For example:

Beverley – I'm really pleased with myself because I've given up smoking.
Bill – Well, at least you have done one good thing this year! (sarcastic)
Beverley – Actually I have done a lot of good things this year. (spoken calmly, statement of fact, not emotionally charged or defensive)

In this true interaction I was able to deal with Bill's putdown because of my belief that I have the right to be treated with respect. If I did not believe it I would be more likely to take his comment as a reflection of me. Something to remember when other people attempt to put you down is that it is a statement about them, not about you. Those who feel secure and have a healthy self-image do not need to put other people down. Let their problem belong to them and do not make it yours.

Whilst believing I have the right to be treated with respect, I also believe that others have the right to respect too. Students sometimes say to me, 'What if someone is aggressive towards you, surely they do not deserve to be treated with respect'. My answer to this is that you do not have to allow someone else's behaviour to dictate yours. If a person is aggressive towards you and you think 'To hell with it, they are being rotten to me, I will be rotten to them' you are, in effect, saying 'You can control my behaviour. The way I behave will depend on the way you behave'. Remember that assertion is self-enhancing behaviour – in other words, it feels good! I find that sufficient reason to attempt to maintain it even when I am not being treated with respect.

I think it is much more difficult to remain assertive in the face of aggression than when dealing with non-assertive or assertive responses from another. However, from my experience of maintaining an assertive stance in the face of aggression, it tends to defuse the other person's angry feelings or, alternatively, they realize they can get nowhere and are likely to withdraw. And, most important, it feels terrific. I have been really pleased with myself on each occasion when I have been able to remain calm in the face of an aggressive attack. I do not mean that I felt superior to the other person – I felt good about my behaviour and my ability to 'act' rather than 'react'.

THE RIGHT TO MAKE MISTAKES

I have already mentioned an example where my belief in my right to make mistakes helped me to be assertive. It enabled me to take responsibility for my actions without becoming defensive or to engage in self-putdowns. We all make mistakes – a fact of life – it is the way we learn. Accept that fact and your own humanness and fallibility, and mistakes then become part of your learning process – not an attack on your self-esteem.

A number of times students have said to me, 'But if I take on the right to make mistakes, I might make them all the time and not care'. This statement indicates a view which is prevalent in our society that we need to be hard on ourselves and keep ourselves in very close check or we will become worse than we are – a touch of the 'monster within' belief. We do not say to children as they are learning to walk, 'You really are useless, that is the fifth time you have fallen down, do it again and I will punish you'. Sounds ridiculous? Of course it is! The child learning to walk does not learn through putdowns, abuse and punishment – they learn through support and encouragement, through seeing the excitement and joy on their parents' faces as they

make their early faltering steps. We would all get
along far better if we were as kind to ourselves and
others when mistakes are made as we are with young
children as they learn to walk. Be gentle with yourself,
support yourself, encourage yourself. We all have a
child inside us who needs to be nurtured.

THE RIGHT TO FAIL

I had tremendous difficulty in accepting this right.
How does it help you to have the right to fail? The
difference it has made to me is that it has enabled me
to attempt things that I am uncertain I will be
successful at. It has made me more able to take risks.
If failure will not destroy me or damage my self-esteem
to any great extent, I will attempt more. At one time I
was afraid to try many things because of the fear of
failure.

Think about failure for a moment. What does it
mean to you? To me it meant lowered self-esteem and
confirmation that I was incapable. Failure at a task
meant failure as a person. You may find this to be a
problem for you too. If you equate failure at something
you have attempted – an exam, a task, a new job, a
relationship – with failure as a person, it will make
taking risks and trying something new more difficult
for you. If failure feels terrible then you will tend to
avoid situations where you might end up feeling this
way.

I was asked to teach assertiveness training four
years ago when I finished university. I had never
taught before and, in fact, I had always been afraid of
talking in front of groups. I decided to take a risk and
accept the offer. I was helped by the fact that the
person who asked me had faith in my ability. Another
friend gave me a few points to remember – 'You know
more than they do about the subject. They are probably
more nervous than you are'. There were other hints but
I do not remember them all. I was a bit nervous when I
went to the first class. I remember having a little

trouble getting my words out for the first five or ten minutes. After that initial period I completely forgot about myself and how I was performing – I just taught. That class was a most enjoyable experience for me and I walked away from the class thinking 'I do not know the person I was in there. This is a facet of my personality I have never seen before'. In order to take on that class I had to be prepared to accept possible failure. It turned out that I have good teaching skills – it could quite easily have gone the other way and that was a possibility I had to be prepared to face. In this situation I was successful – sometimes I am not.

A situation where I was not successful was when I was asked to give a talk on communication. I had felt quite confident that I could do this, based on my experience of teaching and my lack of fear of speaking in public. However, the talk was a flop! I never gained the audience's attention, they fidgeted and talked amongst themselves and at the end they clapped 'politely'. On this occasion I failed to be successful. However, I did learn from this experience – I accepted that I had failed and that I had the right to do so. I did not punish myself for my failure but, instead, looked at where I knew I had gone wrong. I realized I had made the mistake of not knowing my audience – I had thought I would be speaking to a group of women but, in fact, the group were young people of both sexes. I had mistakenly assumed that teaching skills were the same as public speaking skills – they are not. The assertive action which I took on realizing where I had gone wrong was that I took a course in public speaking and acquired the skills I lacked. My belief in the right to fail helped me to learn from the experience – and benefit from it. Unless I am prepared to fail, I will not discover what I can be successful at.

THE RIGHT TO SUCCEED

It may sound strange to follow on the right to fail with the right to succeed, but for many of us the possibility of success is also a problem. It is for me and is something I am working to overcome at present. For me there are many fears attached to success:

- What responsibilities will success bring? Will I be able to handle them?
- Will others (and myself) expect more of me than I am capable of?
- Will men be threatened by me if I am successful? Is success unfeminine?
- Will my friends be happy or envious if I am successful?
- Will my family be happy or envious if I am successful?

Not all these fears are unfounded. Success does bring responsibility; others (and myself) will expect more; sometimes others are envious and do dislike people who are successful; many men are threatened by successful women.

I actually do believe I have the right to be successful and taking on the right has put me in touch with my fears. I needed firstly to believe I had the right before I could take the next step on to facing my fears. Once I have faced them I need to decide whether I am prepared to face the possible repercussions.

THE RIGHT TO EXPRESS MY FEELINGS

I think it is useful when talking about feelings to break them down into individual feelings. Most of us find some feelings more acceptable than others. I will mention just two here.

Anger

At one time I had great difficulty accepting that it was okay to feel angry – and even more difficulty accepting that it was alright to express it. Now, for the most part, anger is acceptable to me. I can feel it and sometimes I express it if it seems appropriate to do so.

I do not feel I have to justify my anger – if I feel angry, I feel angry. I feel freer in my relationships because of this and am more honest with those I am involved with. I tend not to hold my anger inside, letting it fester and building up resentment towards others. Acceptance of the right to feel and express anger has made me a more spontaneous and alive person.

Sadness

Very often seemingly happy events have a component of sadness in them. At one time I found it difficult to accept this paradox and would fight to keep my sadness hidden from my own awareness as well as from others. For example, when I finished university and got my degree, I thought I should be happy. I had been working for this for a long time and had been successful. Part of me was happy, but another part of me was very sad because gaining my degree signalled the end of a period of my life which had been very fulfilling. Once I accepted that it was okay to feel sad as well, I allowed myself to feel it and it passed.

I find it much easier to accept all my feelings now – they are part of a passing parade. I feel them and sometimes I express them to others. I no longer censor them – I believe I have the right to feel and express them.

THE RIGHT NOT TO ASSERT MYSELF

I will finish off with a right which may sound quite strange in a book on assertion. The reason I took on this one was because after doing my first assertion course I became quite compulsive about it and felt I should express my feelings and opinions at all times. I discovered that this was quite exhausting and also unnecessary. Sometimes I just did not feel like standing up for my rights; at other times I did not want to tell a particular person how I felt. Now I am no longer compulsive about assertion – sometimes I choose to be non-assertive – and it feels fine to do so.

YOUR LIST OF PERSONAL RIGHTS

As I said earlier, it is useful to choose your own list of personal rights – ones that have meaning for you. I will list below some which you might find useful and which may stimulate you to think of others:

- to have privacy
- to decide what to do with your time
- to express your opinions
- to hold political beliefs
- to hold religious beliefs
- to cry
- to laugh
- to say you don't know
- to say you don't understand
- to say no
- to have time on your own
- to do nothing
- to change
- to be a vegetarian
- to refuse a drink

When thinking about personal rights, ask yourself, 'How would my life be different if I believed I had the right to . . . . . ?'

Having talked about how taking on certain personal rights has helped me to change, I want to mention that other people also have rights. This may seem obvious but it is something which was not emphasized in the first assertion course I did. The result was that I was very aware of my own rights and tended to forget about other people's. For example, I remember confronting my boss about something I was unhappy about – I took on the right to express my feelings and to ask for what I wanted. However, I did so in such a way that I did not allow him space to express his feelings or say what he wanted. I did not open up communication – I made demands. It is useful to be aware that whilst I have the right 'to ask for what I want', it is *ask* not *demand*. The person I am making the request of has the right to say no. When exercising your personal rights I recommend that you also give thought to the other person. Ask yourself whether you are treating them with the same respect you would like to receive.

10.
SELF-ESTEEM

Self-esteem involves the degree to which I respect myself or have a favourable opinion of myself. There is a relationship between self-esteem and assertive behaviour. If a person has a very low opinion of their worth as a human being, it will be difficult for them to take on personal rights and assert themselves. For example, if I do not believe I am worthwhile, how can I take on the right to be treated with respect? As a person begins to believe they have rights their self-esteem improves. As the belief in their rights improves their self-esteem, they start to behave assertively. As they behave assertively in more situations, so their self-esteem continues to improve. Assertion is self-enhancing behaviour – it feels good – it improves self-esteem. It feels good because when I am behaving assertively I have respect for you as well as for me. Therefore, it is not only self-enhancing – it is also 'other' enhancing. When we treat ourselves and others in this way we give ourselves a self-esteem boost. I see the process as being something like this:

SMALL BELIEF IN RIGHTS AND OWN WORTH . . . SMALL ASSERTIVE RISK . . . RAISED SELF-ESTEEM . . . GREATER BELIEF IN RIGHTS AND OWN WORTH . . . GREATER ASSERTIVE RISK . . . SELF-ESTEEM RAISED FURTHER . . . EVEN GREATER BELIEF IN RIGHTS AND OWN WORTH . . . EVEN GREATER ASSERTIVE RISK . . . SELF-ESTEEM RAISED EVEN FURTHER etc.

ACCEPTANCE

It is not necessary for you or I to be perfect in order to have healthy self-esteem. High self-esteem does not go hand-in-hand with perfection. Having healthy self-esteem means that I accept myself with my successes and failures, with my strengths and weaknesses, with my talents and my shortcomings, with my virtues and my vices. However, many of us do not recognize or acknowledge our positive traits, and we over-emphasize and denigrate ourselves for our negative traits. I am of the firm belief that we do not need the help of anyone else to put us down or criticize us – we are perfectly capable of doing it ourselves. If we are all capable of giving ourselves a difficult time, then it stands to reason that it lies within our power to build ourselves up, to encourage ourselves and to develop our own self-esteem. In fact, I would go so far as to say that it is our responsibility to build our own self-esteem and not to rely on others to do it for us. Certainly, it is wonderful if we get some help along the way – an added bonus; however, if your source of self-esteem lies outside yourself it means that as soon as the other person or persons withdraw their approval or acceptance, your self-esteem will suffer.

When I first heard about the importance of accepting myself as I was, I found the concept difficult. I wanted to improve, to develop and to change. If I accepted myself as I was, how would I be able to change? After all, surely change required that I dislike my faults, vices and shortcomings – if I accepted them why would I bother to change them? There is a paradox involved here – we make deep and meaningful change through acceptance, not criticism or rejection. I will use a personal example. When I was fifteen I worked for a government department in a typing pool. The supervisor constantly criticized my work and typing ability. My work became worse and worse under this barrage of criticism and non-acceptance. Fortunately, I was transferred to another typing pool where the supervisor was encouraging and supportive – the trend reversed and I became better and better at my work. The reference I received from the last secretarial job I held said – 'Beverley's typing skills are the best I have seen in 25 years of public accounting'. I wonder if that would have been the case had I stayed much longer with the original supervisor. I improved through support, encouragement and *acceptance*. This example is a case of someone else not accepting me, but the effect is the same whether it comes from outside or inside. In fact, if you build up your own self-esteem and accept yourself, other people's opinions of you will no longer have the same effect.

IMPROVING SELF-ESTEEM

'Doing' and 'being'

I would like to discuss ways in which you can improve your self-esteem. One way is to start listening to what you are saying to yourself. How often do you tell yourself you are stupid, a failure, selfish, lazy, inefficient, disorganised, unreliable, insensitive, careless, etc., etc.? It is useful to be aware that *doing* is not the same as *being*: I may have behaved in a careless way – that does not make me a careless person. There is a difference between who I am as a person and my behaviour. When you hear yourself saying things which focus on you as a person, change them to statements about behaviour:

> I am stupid.   →What I did was stupid.
> I am inefficient. →I did not perform that test
>   efficiently.
> I am a failure.   →I failed at this exam.

I am responsible for my behaviour, but I am *not* my behaviour. Learn to separate who you *are* from what you *do*.

Be kind to yourself

When you find yourself giving yourself a hard time
about something, say *stop*. When you start up again, as
you undoubtedly will, say *stop* again. Keep saying it
until you have stopped doing it. Learn to be kind to
yourself – to treat yourself as your own best friend.
What would you do if a dear friend were talking to you
about how hopeless he or she feels, how selfish he or
she has been or what a failure he or she is as a person?
Would you sit there and agree – 'Yes, you are pretty
hopeless. Yes, you are selfish and a real failure as
well.'? Or would you support, accept and encourage?
Would you dispute what they are saying about
themselves and point out their good points? Would you
tell them that you value them and think they are
great? If you can do that for a friend – you can do that
for yourself!

Spend some time thinking about yourself and looking
at your positive traits, at your talents and your
successes. It is useful to write a list of what you see as
your positive attributes. You may find it quite difficult
to do at first – not because there are no positives, but
because you may not recognize them as such. Positive
attributes do not have to be earth-shattering things
that would make the newspaper headlines. They can be
simple things like being kind to animals, treating your
environment with care and concern, looking after your
plants, having brought up your children, being able to
listen to others, being able to have fun, etc. You could
perhaps ask a close friend or family member to write
down what they see as your positive attributes – they
may see things you do not see or had not thought of as
positive traits. Keep building on your list of positives.

Be aware also of your negative traits, but do not be
immobilized by them or nag yourself about them. All of
us have negative traits – it is part of the human
condition. If we were perfect we would be gods!

Doing nice things for yourself can enhance self-
esteem. The following are suggestions of some things
you can do for yourself!

- Buy a special outfit.
- Let yourself luxuriate in a hot bath.
- Spend a day in bed reading.
- Have a massage.
- Spend money on your personal development.
- Buy yourself a bunch of flowers.
- Take yourself out to dinner.
- Buy yourself a luxurious gift.
- Have a sauna.
- Visit an art gallery or museum

Treat yourself the way you would treat someone you loved very much and the way in which you would like someone you loved to treat you. You can do it for yourself!

11.
SELF-TALK

Behaving assertively requires that you have a certain
amount of control of yourself. It does not have to be
complete control, but enough to enable you to express
yourself in a way in which you get your message
across. There are certain feelings which, when
experienced in 'excessive' form, cause problems in
behaving assertively. These feelings are excessive
anger, excessive anxiety and depression. If I am feeling
extremely angry with you and I express that anger, I
am likely to behave aggressively. Or if I am
excessively anxious about a situation, I am likely to
behave non-assertively. When I am feeling depressed it
will be difficult for me to express myself in any way.

RATIONAL-EMOTIVE THERAPY

In this first part of the chapter I am going to talk
about Rational-Emotive Therapy (RET) and show how
its principles can be used to deal with feelings and
place them under firmer control. The major premise
which underlies RET is that 'thinking precedes feeling'
and it is not what happens to us which causes us to
feel angry, anxious, sad, hurt, etc., but what we say to
ourselves about what happens. What we say to
ourselves is sometimes called 'self-talk'. For example, I
am driving along one day when another driver turns
right in front of me without indicating. I can get
myself into a rage about the event with this type of
self-talk:

*'What a stupid thing to do. People like that should not
be allowed on the road. Road-hog! Doesn't he know he*

*could cause an accident. People like that are so
inconsiderate. He is probably totally selfish.'*

I have certainly gone through these types of thoughts
at times and ended up feeling extremely angry and
self-righteous. Given the chance to say something to
the person it is likely to be aggressive – 'Don't you
have any indicators, stupid?'. It is not the event that
caused the emotion of anger, it is my thoughts or 'self-
talk'.

I will do a re-run of the same situation of the car
failing to indicate. I can remain calmer with this type
of self-talk:

*'That gave me a fright, it would have been better if he
had indicated to let me know he was going right. I do
feel a bit shaken up. Still, we all make mistakes. I have
probably done it myself at times.'*

The resultant emotion is unlikely to be very strong and
I will soon forget about the event. I find that when I
work myself up into a very angry state I do not forget
about the situation quickly. It runs around in my head
causing me a great deal of discomfort, and wastes my
time and energy which could be put to far more
constructive use.

In RET it is claimed that we have the capacity to
think in three different ways:

- rationally
- irrationally
- rationalizing

Rational thinking is when we accept reality and are
not *demanding* that things be different to the way
they are. We may prefer that things be different, but
we do not get into a rage when our desires are not met.
For example, in the situation already mentioned a
rational belief about it would be 'I prefer it when other
drivers indicate to let me know what they are doing'. I

do not *demand* that things be different to the way they are. I accept reality. The reality of this situation is that people make mistakes when they are driving.

Irrational thinking is when we do not like or accept reality and *demand* that people, life, the world, be different to the way they are. Using the same example, an irrational belief would be 'Other drivers *should* always indicate when turning'. This is a refusal to accept reality. Again, the reality is that people make mistakes. With this belief the person is, in effect, saying 'I do not like reality – it *should* be different'.

Rationalizing is when we pretend that things do not bother us. Using the driving example, I may feel scared but I rationalize the feeling away by saying something like 'That didn't bother me'. Or, to use another example, I may feel hurt by you ignoring me but I rationalize the feeling by saying 'I didn't really like him anyway'. In both cases I am lying to myself to avoid dealing with my real feelings.

It is important to be aware that RET is not about repression of feelings. I would never support a theory which suggested such a course of action. It is concerned with toning down emotions which make it difficult to perform effectively. This requires that you experience, accept and recognize the emotion. Sometimes you will have to work backwards – you will find yourself very angry and then need to listen to the self-talk which is creating the emotion. It is only when you have done this that you will be able to work at toning it down.

In order to use this theory you need to be aware of the process:

EVENT . . . SELF-TALK . . . EMOTION

To begin with you will probably find you are experiencing an excessive emotion and be unaware of how it has happened. You can then start listening to yourself and become aware of the self-talk. However, it is not sufficient to merely recognize what you are saying to yourself – you need to change the irrational thinking by challenging it. I will use a personal example to explain how this works:

Event – A friend did something which I thought was nasty.
Emotion – I felt excessively angry with her. I spent several days in a rage with her feeling indignant and self-righteous. My awareness was:

Event → *Emotion*
(Friend being nasty)   (Excessive anger)

I was unaware of the middle step – self-talk. After a few days I got tired of feeling so angry – I was consumed by my rage and it was taking over a large part of my waking thoughts. I realized it was time for me to listen to what I was saying to myself to create the anger. This is what I heard:

'What a rotten person she is. Imagine doing that to a friend. Friends should not behave that way. She is obviously not a real friend or she would not do something like that. How dare she do that. What a bitch she is. etc. etc.'

No wonder I was so angry! Now I had awareness of the three steps:

EVENT . . . SELF-TALK . . . EMOTION

However, that awareness was not sufficient to change the feeling. I could hear what I was saying but I was still in a rage with her. There is another step involved in changing the emotion – disputing or challenging the thoughts:

EVENT . . . SELF-TALK . . . EMOTION . . .
CHALLENGE . . . NEW EMOTION

I will go through my thoughts and show you how I challenged them:

Thought	Challenge
Friends should not behave that way.	Why not? Who says friends must always behave the way I think they should?
She's obviously not a real friend or she would not do something like that.	Okay, she has done something I do not like, but does that mean she is not a real friend? She has also done numerous nice things for me.
What a rotten person she is.	Does one nasty act make her a rotten person. I do not like what she has done, but does that make her rotten?
What a bitch she is.	Does one nasty act make her a bitch? Maybe she did not mean to be nasty and, if she did, don't we all do nasty things to others at times.
Imagine doing that to a friend.	Maybe she is not perfect. Does not being perfect mean she is not a real friend.

What happened at the end of this process was that I felt much calmer. I was still angry but my anger was manageable. The basic irrational belief underlying my rage was 'Friends *should* not do nasty things to me'. A rational belief would be 'I would prefer it if friends did not do nasty things'. It may sound as though I am just playing with words by changing 'should' to 'prefer', but I am in fact doing much more than that. I am not merely changing words, I am also changing my attitude. When I say 'Friends *should* . . . .' I am saying 'I do not like reality, it *should* be different'. I may as well stamp my feet and jump up and down like a child. When I say 'I would *prefer* . . .' I am not demanding that reality be different. I accept it – and I would rather it were different. The emotional impact is not the same.

Some irrational beliefs are more deep seated than others and the more strongly we hold the belief, the harder it is to change it. In the example I have just given you I had a deeply held belief about the way friends '*should* be'. Because of this it was quite difficult for me to change my feelings for any length of time. As I said, I reduced my anger to a manageable level, but I was not able to do so for long. In a very short time I was back to ranting and raving to myself about the unfairness of the situation and about the way things '*should* be'. I went through the process of challenging my self-talk a number of times before I was calm long enough to be able to talk about it with my friend. My experience went something like this:

EVENT . . . SELF-TALK . . . EXCESSIVE ANGER . . . CHALLENGE . . . MANAGEABLE ANGER . . .RE-PLAYING EVENT . . . SELF-TALK . . . EXCESSIVE ANGER . . . CHALLENGE . . . MANAGEABLE ANGER etc.

However, eventually I succeeded in reducing my anger to a manageable level and was able to deal with the situation assertively. I told her how I felt without blame – and opened up communication in such a way that she was able to tell me her perception of what had happened. We were able to deal with the situation in a constructive way.

If I had approached her when I was excessively angry I would have blamed her for my feelings, my confrontation would have been aggressive, and I would have caused damage to the relationship. If I had not dealt with my anger using the RET formula and had decided not to tell her how I felt, the relationship would have been damaged by emotional withdrawal and my resentment coming out as passive-aggression.

In the RET theory the claim is that there are a number of ways in which we can cause problems for ourselves:

- demanding
- catastrophizing
- damnation

Demanding is often indicated by the word *must, should* and *ought*. My demand would have been something like 'My friends *must* behave the way I want them to. She *should* do what I want. She *ought* to be different'.

Catastrophizing involves such words as *awful, horrible* and *dreadful*. My catastrophizing would have been 'It is really *awful (horrible/dreadful)* when friends behave this way'. Try saying to yourself 'It is really awful' and then replace it with 'I do not like it when this happens'. Do you find yourself having a different emotional reaction? The situations we label as awful, dreadful and horrible are experienced that way because of the labels – change the label and you change the emotional experience.

Damnation is when you damn someone for their behaviour. That 'someone' can be either yourself or another. The damnation part of my example was statements like 'What a rotten person she is. What a bitch she is'. I am damning the whole person. I am saying she behaved a certain way, therefore, she deserves to be damned/punished for it!

The same process can be applied to situations where excessive anxiety is involved to reduce the anxiety to a manageable level. For example, a couple of years ago I received a phone call asking me to give a talk on communication to a large group of businessmen. I agreed to do so and when I put the phone down I found that my hands were shaking. Being a fairly strong indicator of anxiety, I listened to what I was saying to myself and this is what I heard:

'What if I mumble my words. What if I fall over getting onto the stage. What if I forget what I am saying. What if they are bored. What if . . . What if . . . What if . . .'

This is a perfect example of catastrophizing at its worst. Thinking of every possible negative outcome and getting myself into a state of extreme anxiety. Again, recognizing what I was saying was not sufficient to change my feelings – I needed to challenge them:

Thought	Challenge
What if I mumble my words?	Yes, it is possible that I could mumble my words. In fact, sometimes I mumble them in my classes. It could happen. But it is not the end of the world, I will not be devastated by it. I may feel slightly uncomfortable, but I can do the same as I do in classes and say, 'Excuse me, I have mumbled my words. I will start again.'
What if I fall over getting onto the stage?	What is the likelihood that I will fall over? I have never fallen over going into a class and I do not tend to be particularly clumsy. Of course, it is not out of the realms of possibility that it could happen. Suppose it does – is it a catastrophy? Could I handle the situation? Yes I could. It could be turned into a joke and help to relax the atmosphere. Besides which, people are more likely to feel some sympathy for me than they are to be ridiculing.

Thought	Challenge
What if I forget what I am saying?	It is possible this could happen but I know from experience that I do not need to cover it up or pretend. I can say I have had a mental block – I also know from experience that is the best way of clearing a block.
What if they are bored?	It is possible they may be bored. Unlike people who choose to come to my classes, they may not be interested in interpersonal communication. I can prepare the talk with this in mind and attempt to gain their interest. I will not feel very comfortable if they are bored, but I can live with it if they are. I am prepared to take the risk.

By the time I had finished challenging all my thoughts I was quite calm. Due to the fact that these irrational thoughts were fairly superficial, I did not have to go through the process over and over again as I did with the previous example. Given the same situation a few years ago I would have found it more difficult, but my teaching experience enabled me to work through it quite quickly. You will notice that the challenges are quite realistic – they look at realistic possible outcomes. It is not a matter of telling yourself everything will be just fine.

I have found the RET theory extremely useful in my own life and use it when I am faced with uncomfortable emotions. I will confess that when I first read about the theory, I had some difficulty relating to it. However, a few years later when I read about it again, I found it had a lot of meaning for me. Since it is possible that you may experience the same difficulty as I did when first faced with RET, I am going to discuss another way of looking at emotions which I have also found most useful.

ADDICTION AND PREFERENCE

In his book, *A Conscious Person's Guide to Relationships*, Ken Keyes claims that if we get very upset about anything, we have an addiction to it. People are not only addicted to cigarettes, alcohol or drugs, but also to such things as punctuality, reliability, honesty, tidiness, etc. The problem with addictions is that they are very uncomfortable if they are not satisfied. Just as I may get very twitchy if I do not have a cigarette fix, so I will get extremely agitated if my addiction to punctuality is not satisfied. He claims that if you can change your addiction to a preference you will spend a lot less time being upset. Think for a moment about what a preference is and why it is far more comfortable to live with than an addiction. I have a preference for brown bread and am not so keen on white. However, I am not addicted to brown bread. I have not got to have it. I will not crave it or be enraged if I do not get it. I can live quite comfortably with my preferences – they do not cause me emotional discomfort.

A past addiction which I have upgraded to a preference was an addiction to punctuality in social situations. If I made an arrangement with a friend for a particular time and they were late, I was furious. I tried many ways of dealing with my anger – pretending to myself that I was not angry by rationalizing away the feeling, knowing I was angry but not expressing it directly, demanding that a friend be on time 'or else', making passive-aggressive digs about their tardiness, assertively requesting a friend to be on time. I had success with some people, but life being the way it is and people being the way they are, there were times when people were impunctual. Being an addiction it meant that I could have my mood and evening ruined at any time. With one particular friend who was notoriously impunctual, I went so far as to be angry even before she was late because I was sure she would be! My evenings with her were often ruined even when she was on time. I decided I had had enough of this addiction which was causing me so much discomfort. As with the RET model, I started listening to what I was saying with a particular friend. This is what I heard:

'She should be on time. She should be more reliable. She is hopeless. She does not care about me. If I were important enough she would be on time.'

Again I challenged my thoughts:

Thought	Challenge
She should be on time.	Why should she? Who says so? Is being late such a terrible thing? What is ten minutes? If I were not so agitated I would be able to use the time to relax.
She should be more reliable.	Why should she? Anyway it is my judgement that being late means being unreliable. It could easily be equated with being relaxed and easy going. She is relaxed and easy going and that is one of the reasons I love her. She is extremely reliable in many important things.

Thought	Challenge
She is hopeless.	Is she? She is late – I do not think that makes her hopeless.
She does not care about me.	Doesn't she? What about the many caring things she has done in the years we have known each other. How about the time when I went to university as a full-time student and she gave me a gift of $1,000 when finances were tight. Is that a person who does not care about me.
If I was important enough she would be on time.	Is that true? Isn't she late for everyone? She has not just selected me to be impunctual for, and always being impunctual doesn't mean that nobody is important to her either. That is obviously not true.

This particular friend was not the only one I had difficulty with in regard to punctuality, but working on this had an effect on all the others. The issue of punctuality used to cause me so much unhappiness, but once I took responsibility for *my* problem and stopped blaming others, I was able to do something about it. It took time and effort but it has been well worth it. I still prefer people to be on time. I do not particularly enjoy waiting, but I can live with it quite easily because I am no longer addicted to it.

No matter how assertive you become, you will not get all your needs met all the time. As pointed out earlier assertion is not about 'winning' at other people's expense, nor is it about getting your own way all the time. You can ask for what you want from others (assertion) but they may not always respond to your needs. That is their right – the right to choose whether they will meet your needs or not. Both the RET and Ken Keyes theories can help to tone down emotions in order that you can express yourself assertively. Taking it a step further, they can help you to change yourself when other's refuse to change their behaviour.

MEETING NEEDS

Of course, there is a correlation between being involved in a friendship, marriage or other type of relationship, and meeting needs and having needs met. If you are in a job and you do not meet with your employer's needs, you are likely to have your services dispensed with. I believe the same applies to all relationships. If a friend refuses to meet a large number of my needs the question I ask myself is 'What is the cost of this relationship? Am I paying too high a price for involvement with this person? How many of my needs am I sacrificing? Am I giving up too much of myself?'. These are sometimes difficult and painful questions to ask, but they often need to be asked. I see the process in a relationship as something like this:

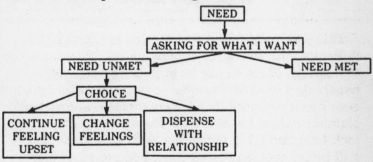

In the situation with my friend I had three choices:

- To continue being angry over her lateness.
- To work at changing my feelings (addiction).
- To end the relationship because it was not worth the angry feelings.

I decided that I did not want to continue being angry every time we saw each other. I also decided that I valued the relationship highly and that the positives far outweighed the negatives. I then decided I would choose the second option and change my feelings.

None of us need be the 'victim' of other people or of our emotions. We have a choice whether or not we decide to stay involved in relationships, and we have a choice about either staying with uncomfortable emotions – or doing something to change them. We are really very powerful people!

12.
SELF-AWARENESS

'GOOD' AND 'BAD' FEELINGS

As stated before, assertion involves the honest expression of feelings. Unfortunately, this is not a simple matter because many people are out of touch with themselves, are unaware of their feelings and are not fully conscious or fully alive. One of the reasons for this is that most of us have been taught that some feelings are 'good' and some feelings are 'bad'. To complicate matters even further we have learned that some are 'good' if you are a woman, but 'bad' if you are a man, and vice versa. Since most of us actually desire to be 'good', we learn to repress the feelings that are labelled 'bad' and unacceptable. However, the repression of feelings will not make them disappear – buried feelings are buried alive. Buried feelings are far more difficult to deal with because if we refuse to recognise them for what they are, they become distorted.

Distorting feelings

I will give you a couple of examples of feelings becoming distorted: John and Anne are at a party together and they start talking to another man, Peter. Peter and Anne discover they have an interest in common and become very involved in their conversation. John notices Anne is very animated, is obviously enjoying herself and he feels left out and jealous. However, he has learned that it is not okay for him to feel jealous – it does not fit into his 'ideal'

image of what a man *should* be. He represses his
jealousy. He starts to find fault with what Anne is
saying and makes derogatory remarks about her
opinions. Anne begins to feel uncomfortable and hurt,
she says less, her animation and enjoyment disappear.
John has achieved what he wanted in terms of putting
a stop to a situation which was making him feel
uncomfortable.

If John had been able to accept that it was okay for
him to feel jealous he would have been able to deal
with the situation in a more constructive and honest
way. With acceptance that he was feeling left out and
jealous he would have been able to decide what to do
with it. He may have decided he was not prepared to
express his feelings to Anne and Peter and, instead,
either tried to come to terms with the emotion, or have
suggested that he would like to join in the conversation
and could they talk about something else. He could
also have told Anne later that he was feeling jealous
and left out and the real issue could have been dealt
with. The problem with the repression and subsequent
distortion of feelings is that the real issue does not get
addressed. The problem gets pushed aside until it
arises again, as it undoubtedly will. Also, John's
downgrading of Anne is likely to leave her feeling
resentful and angry. A happy evening is spoiled.

Men are not the only ones who repress and distort
feelings – women are just as capable of this behaviour.
Karen is spending the day with her mother whom she
loves dearly. Her mother starts nagging Karen about
her excess weight, assuring her that she is only
thinking of her own good and how much better she
would feel if she lost a stone. Karen feels stirrings of
anger towards her mother, but anger is not acceptable
to her – she loves her mother. She quickly represses
the emotion and submissively agrees with her mother
that she could do with losing some weight. Later on in
the day Karen picks on one of her mother's weak spots
(which our nearest and dearest know only too well)
telling her mother that it really is time she cut down

on her smoking and, of course, she is only thinking of her welfare in saying this!

Had Karen been able to accept her anger towards her mother she would have been able to do something about it. Like John she may not wish to tell her mother she is angry but, rather, to deal with the emotion herself. Or, she could tell her mother she knows she is overweight and does not wish to discuss it any further, thereby putting a stop to the conversation she feels uncomfortable with. Or, she may wish to tell her mother how angry she feels when she brings up the subject of her weight. The real problem is dealt with rather than buried.

Feelings are amoral

I want to present the idea of feelings being amoral – meaning that they have no moral value whatsoever. Having no moral value they can be labelled neither good nor bad – they just 'are'. As human beings we have access to an incredible range of emotions from love to hate, joy to despair, boredom to excitement, frustration to exhilaration – to name but a few. How many of us allow ourselves to experience the whole spectrum that is available to us? There are other reasons besides the morality of feelings which causes us to avoid them, like avoiding feeling excited for fear of being disappointed or avoiding love for fear of being hurt. However, the labels of 'good' and 'bad' are one of the reasons for repression and it is worthwhile looking at this.

In presenting the idea that feelings are amoral, I would point out that I am talking only of feelings – not actions. My feeling of hate for you may be amoral – my action of sticking a knife in your back is not. There is a difference between feelings and actions. What you do with a particular feeling may have a quite significant moral value! If you can accept feelings as having no moral value, it will be easier for you to feel them and then decide what to do with them. If you repress your feelings you are not aware of them, and in not being aware of how you feel in any given situation you will be unable to make decisions in possession of all the facts. We are feeling as well as thinking beings – to base our decisions on reason and logic alone is to deny a large component of ourselves.

GETTING IN TOUCH WITH YOUR FEELINGS

There was a time in my life when I was very uncomfortable being alone for any length of time. I was afraid of my thoughts and my feelings and did not want to know about them. I kept myself busy, I spent most of my time with others, I avoided my 'self'. I think the hardest thing for many of us to do is to confront ourselves – the reason being that we are terrified of what we shall find. Carl Rogers refers to it as fear of the 'beast within'. Now I love to be alone, my quiet times to myself are very precious to me and I feel fragmented and cheated at times when circumstances make it difficult for me to take time out on my own. I am no longer afraid of my thoughts and feelings, I see them now as part of the passing parade of myself as a process. I am not a static entity, even my physical body is changing and renewing itself constantly – the skin I have today is not the same skin I had last year. So it is with my thoughts and feelings – they pass and they change. I have discovered that there is no 'beast within' and most of the time I am comfortable with myself.

Of course, there are times when I do not want to face my feelings, when I become agitated and uncomfortable, when I find it difficult to concentrate or to meditate. This has happened to me from time to time whilst writing this book – it happened yesterday. I became blocked, unable to write, restless and lacking in concentration. I decided that what I had written so far was a load of rubbish and that I did not really want to write a book at all. Eventually I realized what it was all about. I had read an article in *The Sunday Times* about a woman called Kay Lily who teaches assertiveness training in London, and had been angered by the way the reporter represented both Kay Lily and assertiveness training. This fed into my fears of going into print, being open to criticism on a large scale, being misunderstood and being misrepresented by the media. I was scared! Once I faced my anger towards the reporter and my fears about writing a book, I was able to deal with my feelings and get on with my writing. Today my writing is flowing easily, I am calm and relaxed, my concentration level is high, I like what I have written and I most certainly do want to write this book!

You may be thinking it is all very fine for her talking about self-awareness and getting in touch with feelings, but 'How do I do it?'. The first step is to start listening to yourself, and to ask yourself 'How do I feel about this situation? What is really going on for me?'. There was a time when I was sharing a house with someone who was sick for a large part of the time and I felt I should do more of the chores than she did (please note the 'should'). I told myself I did not mind – after all, it would be extremely selfish not to help a poor sick person. However, I realized that she managed to be well enough to do things she liked doing and also that she would do nothing constructive to help herself. Feelings of discomfort started to surface. I began asking myself each time I took out the rubbish bag or took her clothes off the line or did the washing-up she had left. 'How do I feel about doing this?'. At first the answer that came back was 'Fine. I do not mind helping her'. After a while the answer came back with a resounding 'Yes, I do mind. I feel extremely resentful and angry that so much of my time goes into supporting Carol'. At last I was in touch with the 'real' feelings – the ones that I considered were not 'nice'! Once in touch with them I was able to do something about the situation because I was in possession of all the 'facts'. I was not able to communicate honestly and openly or, in other words, assertively, until I knew how I was really feeling.

Ways of becoming more self-aware

Another way of becoming more self-aware which I have
found useful is to write. If I am concerned about
something but am confused about how I feel, I ask
myself on paper and then scribble away anything that
comes into my head. I do not censor it in any way. The
page will not judge me and when I am finished I can
tear it up and throw it away. I have often found some
clarity about my feelings by doing this.

By far the most powerful way I have found to become
more aware is by talking to someone about it. It
requires a special sort of person to be able to do this
with. A person who will listen and not judge, listen and
not offer advice and listen and accept your feelings in a
way that perhaps you are not fully able to accept them
yourself. The person who can do this is a gem beyond
value, because not only do they help you to become
more self-aware but they also help you to accept
yourself and your feelings.

My first experience of this kind of acceptance was
when I was training to be a telephone counsellor with
Lifeline in Sydney, Australia. The training lasted six
months and I vividly remember the drive home from
our last session during which we had said what we felt
about each other. During my training I had told them
things about myself and my feelings that I had never
told anyone before because I was sure people would
never like me if they knew what I was really like.
Driving home I remember the wonder and amazement
I felt to realize that these people with whom I had
bared my soul and revealed my true self could still care
about me and think I was terrific. I think that
realization was one of the most significant moments of
my life. From there I have never looked back.

In the past ten years I have had friends with whom I
have been able to do this same thing. I have not felt
free to discuss all my feelings with all my friends –
with one I may feel free to share one aspect, with
another a different aspect. I have had outlets with
caring people who have helped me to develop as a

person. When there was something I found too difficult to talk out with a friend, I would see a counsellor. Because of my close relationships with friends it was sometimes necessary to talk with someone more detached, someone without a vested interest. It is not possible for us to always be available to our nearest and dearest in a way which is necessary to promote growth since at times we may be threatened by their development. If you do not have the sort of friend you feel free to express yourself with, it may be helpful to find a counsellor who is trained to listen.

HANDLING FEELINGS

I have talked about ways of raising your awareness of your feelings. The next step is 'What do I do with the feeling now I know what it is?'. The purpose of becoming more conscious of feelings is to release them, not hold onto them or 'wallow' in them. If I discover that I have feelings of intense anger towards someone, I will do myself as much harm by hanging onto the feeling as I will by repressing it. I have already given you some information about how to tone down your feelings by listening to your self-talk. Once at a manageable level assertion comes into play. You will be able to release many of your feelings through talking to the person involved about it. I have often found that doing this resolves the feeling and the situation. However, there are many times and situations in which it is not appropriate to tell the person concerned. Remember that assertion involves appropriateness. For example, it may not be appropriate to tell your sick 80-year-old father that you resent something he did when you were a child.

Five years after my husband and I separated he remarried. Much to my amazement I was extremely upset when I heard the news. Part of me was really pleased for him and wished him well – and I communicated this to him by writing a letter. There was another part of me that was quite shattered by the news. It brought up feelings of sadness, guilt and failure. There were things I needed to say that I had never said to him. I felt it was quite inappropriate for me to say these things to him on the 'eve of his marriage' when he was starting a new life. What was I to do? I felt I could be free of the feelings if I were able to express them to him. What I did was to write him a long letter saying all the things I needed so much to say. Many of these feelings were warm and sad, others were angry – I let it all pour out onto several pages. When I had finished writing I felt so much better – I felt released from the past. That was the last time I experienced intense emotions about my husband and our marriage – the letter resolved my feelings. I never sent that letter – it was not necessary to do so. If you have unresolved feelings about someone you can release them by writing to them. Whether you post the letter or not is irrelevant. Sometimes it is inappropriate to express your feelings directly to the person involved and if it is, then this is a very effective way of releasing your feelings.

Another thing I do sometimes when I feel really angry is to beat up my pillows and say whatever I want to say, letting it all go. Afterwards I usually feel much calmer and I also often find that beneath the anger is another emotion. Like yesterday when I was restless and unable to write. The first emotion I came in touch with was anger so I beat up my pillows and released the anger. After I had released the anger I found that the underlying feeling was the fear which I have already told you about.

Some people find sport a useful way of releasing emotions. I was playing squash with a friend who was feeling extremely frustrated and angry with her husband and son. Each time she hit the ball she would say, 'That's Tom!' or 'That's Bill!'. By the end of the game she felt much more able to go home and even felt quite warm towards them. We all get frustrated with those we love and there is no harm in releasing it in this way. The possible negative results of not releasing it are far greater. It is up to each person to decide for themselves when it is appropriate to express their feelings directly to the person concerned and when it is more appropriate to release them some other way.

Repressing emotions

The repression of feelings is unhealthy. It stands to reason that if you spend a great deal of time squashing your feelings, it is going to require a lot of energy to do so. For example, anger has physiological as well as psychological effects – my body will get ready to take action, either to fight or to flee when I feel angry. If I deny the anger and do not allow it to have expression, it will have negative effects on both body and mind. It is claimed that some physical illnesses such as ulcers, migraine headaches and even cancer are the result of repressed emotions. Our bodies and minds are not separate entities, they interact with and affect each other.

You may identify with the pressure cooker effect that can happen when you try to ignore or push away a feeling. Perhaps you are irritated with your spouse because she always leaves you to empty the rubbish. You tell yourself you do not really mind doing it even though you feel stronger and stronger stirrings of emotion inside. One day you explode into rage – 'You are really selfish. You expect me to help you with things around the house and I am doing more than my share. When was the last time you emptied the rubbish?' It is not one occasion that has resulted in the aggressive attack – it is numerous occasions. Each time the anger has been denied and pushed away until one day the lid on the pressure cooker blows off. The spouse on the receiving end of this attack is likely to be stunned by it. The reason being that she did not know you were building up so much anger. We are not mind readers. If something upsets, angers or hurts you, tell the other person. They will not be able to meet your needs unless they know what they are.

115

In order to communicate our feelings and needs to others, we need to know what they are. It is each person's responsibility to know what they feel and to communicate those feelings to the people with whom they interact.

13.
VICTIM CONSCIOUSNESS

This chapter has been the most difficult one for me to write. Whenever I thought about it my mind would go blank and no ideas were forthcoming. In fact, I finished all the other chapters and decided that perhaps this one would have to be scrapped. I could not understand why I was coming against such a total blank since I think it is important to understand how victim consciousness plays such a crucial role in whether we feel in control of our own lives or not. I felt it was a very important part of this book. Then the penny dropped – the blank was connected to the fact that during the writing of this book I have been trying to come to terms with areas of my life where I feel a victim. Writing about it felt just a little too close to home for comfort – and so I blanked out on the whole subject area. The writing of this book has been, like most other experiences in my life, an opportunity for self-development and, as I have said earlier, self-development involves confrontation with 'self'. The part of my 'self' I was not prepared to confront and deal with through the writing of this chapter was that part which still believes I am a victim.

BEING A VICTIM VS. TAKING RESPONSIBILITY

What does it mean to believe I am a victim? It means that in certain areas I feel I have no choice, or that I am not in control of a situation. Victim consciousness involves feelings of powerlessness. All of us feel we are victims to some degree in our lives, and those are the areas where we disempower ourselves. If I feel powerless or helpless in a situation, my ability to do something about that situation is diminished. If I am prepared to give up the victim act and take responsibility for my situation, then I can take action and do something to change it, or accept that this is the way things are and take responsibility for the choice to stay in a particular situation.

'Victim' thinking

The truth of the matter is that in every situation we find ourselves in, we have a choice. However, we often deny that there is any choice, refuse to take responsibility for where we find ourselves and feel powerless to change the situation. For example, a man is working at a job he hates but he believes he has no choice but to stay in that job because he has a wife and three children to support. The real situation is that he *does* have a choice, but that he may not like the other alternatives. He could leave his job and get another (maybe with less pay, worse conditions, etc.), he could suggest to his wife that they reverse roles and she works while he looks after the children or he could go on the dole. There are lots of alternatives. If I were to suggest to such a person that he has a choice, he would probably deny it by saying, 'Yes, but . . .' The fact is that he has made a choice to stay in the job because he does not like the alternatives. In the process of making that choice he has denied that he has made one. The fact that we do not like the alternatives in a situation does not alter the fact that we have made a choice.

If a person can accept that he or she has made a choice in any given situation, then their feelings about the situation will change. If the man in the above example would accept his choice and take responsibility for his decision then his inner thoughts about such a situation will change from:

'I really hate this job. It's awful that I have to stay in it.

I wish I could do something different. I'm trapped. I have no choice. I have to support my wife and kids. Isn't life awful.'

to:

'I hate this job. What are the alternatives? There are not many jobs around at the moment so my chances of finding one that pays as well are very slim. However, I could keep looking at the papers and see what I can find. Or, I could talk to Karen about reversing roles for a while. She may not earn as much as me but we could look at that possibility. Or, I could resign and go on the dole. It would mean selling the house and moving to a less expensive area. I feel my health is suffering and I will not be much use to the family if I have a breakdown. I need to weigh up what is important to me and make a choice based on that.'

Once a person's thinking changes from that of 'victim' to that of choice and responsibility, the feelings also change. The person who accepts that their life involves a series of choices, some more difficult than others, uses their own personal power. They come from a position of strength rather than one of weakness.

Choosing your role

I will now use two examples of my own, which were happening while I was writing this book, to illustrate my point further. As I have said earlier, I returned to England from Australia in September 1986. The adjustment to life in England has proven to be far more difficult than I had anticipated and I have experienced strong feelings of homesickness for Australia. In that time I have often felt the desire simply to pack my bags and go home to Sydney. However, for much of the time I have not seen myself as having a choice because of my mother. These are the types of thoughts that have gone through my mind:

'I can't go back to Sydney because Mum would be

terribly upset. It would be awful of me to leave her now as Dad only died eight months ago and she's never been alone in her life before. I can't leave her in the winter because that would be too hard on her. If I'm going, I have to wait at least until spring or summer. I'd feel terrible about leaving her. I have no choice but to stay.'

This is all 'victim' thinking and resulted in me feeling not only powerless but also resentful towards my mother. What I was doing was blaming her for my feelings. I will show you how each thought can be changed to one of choice and responsibility:

Victim	Choice
I can't go back to Sydney because Mum would be terribly upset.	Mum would be very upset if I decided to go back to Sydney. I have great difficulty seeing Mum upset and I fear the guilt I will feel if I make a decision to return there.
It would be awful of me to leave her now as Dad died only eight months ago and she's never been alone in her life before.	I know it would be difficult for Mum if I were to decide to go. She is still adjusting to Dad's death and has not yet got used to being on her own. I feel concerned at the thought of her being alone.

Victim	Choice
I can't leave her before the winter because that would be too hard on her. If I'm going I at least have to wait until Spring or Summer.	Winter is rather long and depressing in England. I do not like the idea of leaving her alone before the winter is over. If I decide to go I will do so in Spring or Summer. I would feel more comforable about that.
I'd feel terrible about leaving her.	It would be difficult to leave Mum and I know I would miss her and feel very sad not to be with her.
I have no choice but to stay.	I know I need to come to terms with my feelings of guilt. Once I am able to do that it will be easier for me to make a choice about what is best for me. I will, of course, consider Mum in the decision making, but if I make a choice to stay it must be because I want to and not because I feel too guilty to leave. A decision based on guilt would result in our relationship being damaged. I do not want that to happen.

You will notice that in contrast to 'victim' thinking which focuses on the other person and their feelings, making a choice involves concentrating on your own feelings. I need to accept that the problem for me is not my mother being upset – the problem is about how *I feel* when she is upset.

My relationship with my mother has changed since we have both started to take less responsibility for each other. I have talked to her about returning to Australia – and she has told me how she feels about it. At one time she would *not* have said how she felt for fear of putting pressure on me or making me feel guilty. When she said she did feel very upset and was praying for a miracle that would make me stay, I felt incredibly guilty. I feel less guilty now and, as a result, she feels freer to express her feelings. Mum is taking less responsibility for my guilt feelings – and I am taking less responsibility for her feeling upset. It is only in this way that honest communication can take place in any relationship. Having worked through my victim feelings about this situation, I now feel that I am able to make a free choice and will be able to handle any feelings arising from that choice.

The other area of my life in which I was feeling a 'victim' was in relation to my body. I stopped smoking almost two years ago and within a year had gained nearly two stone in weight. Like many ex-smokers I replaced cigarettes with food. I ate more and also my metabolic rate had slowed down, so the food did not burn up so quickly. I was feeling powerless and a complete victim to my body. I did not like having the extra weight but felt that no matter what I did I was stuck with it! Then, I decided I was fed up and was going to do something constructive. I joined a slimming club, started counting calories and, of course, I am now losing weight.

I have realized recently that although I knew 'intellectually' that weight is determined by calorie intake and energy used, I have never really accepted that at 'gut' level. I have never felt fully in control of my body. Now I have realized that I do have control of my body, that it is within my power to decide how fat or thin I am going to be. I accept the body I have may not be able to take in as many calories as some other people's bodies; I accept that my food intake as a non-smoker will have to be less than when I was a smoker; I accept that I will always have to watch what I eat in order to have the body size I want. That is the reality! Once again I will show you the two types of thinking involved:

Victim	Choice
I wish I hadn't gained so much weight since I stopped smoking.	Obviously I have replaced cigarettes with food and if I want to be slim again, I need to cut down on what I am eating.
My metabolic rate has slowed down and that's what is making me get so fat. I wish it were not hard.	My metabolic rate has slowed down since I stopped smoking. If I want to remain a non-smoker and I want to be slim, I shall have to cut down on my food intake to less than when I smoked.
It's not fair. I suppose I will have to take up smoking if I want to stay slim.	It would be easier to stay slim if I smoked, but I do not want to smoke again. I will have to accept that one of the drawbacks is that I cannot eat the same as I used to and stay at the weight I want to be.

I suppose I'm doomed to be a slim smoker or a fat non-smoker.	The way I want to be is a slim non-smoker. To achieve that I will need to be more self-disciplined about my eating habits.
It's hopeless.	I choose to work at being slim.

The role of victim is a very seductive one because when I am playing that role I do not have to take responsibility for my actions. I can sit back and complain about how dreadful things are and how difficult life is. I do not have to do anything about it. Seductive though this role is, it leaves us feeling powerless and unable to change situations. We all have the choice as to whether we remain 'victims' or whether we become the 'masters' of our lives.

14.
THE MIND AS A TOOL FOR CHANGE

There are a number of methods for change available besides the 'conscious' method of attempting to change behaviour. By 'conscious' I mean working on the level of behaviour in a direct sense. For example, in learning to say no to others when you do not want to do something, you may make a 'conscious' decision that next time you are asked to babysit or loan money or go out to dinner etc., you will take the risk and say no. It will be a 'conscious' decision to change your behaviour. Another way in which change can be made is through the use of the mind. There are techniques for relaxing the mind (and the body) and also techniques for using the mind for change, some of which I describe in this chapter. I believe the mind is an absolute powerhouse which we do not utilize for our own benefit. We can create the person we wish to be and the life we wish to lead through the use of our minds.

RELAXATION

We live in an extremely fast changing society which places heavy demands upon us. People often find it difficult to deal with certain situations because they are highly stressed and unable to cope effectively with that stress. Stress in itself is neither good nor bad – it is how we manage it that is important. Using relaxation techniques is one way to cope with stress and reduce it to manageable levels. Our ability to be assertive will rest to a certain degree on how calm we feel. You all will have experienced times when your nerves feel so jangled that you fly off the handle very easily. You may also have experienced times when you feel calm and well able to cope with most things that occur. Regular practice of relaxation will enable you to feel calm more often. It is within your power to change your ability to deal with stressful situations.

Different people respond well to different types of relaxation. Some will prefer the more physical types, such as working through the body tensing and then relaxing the different parts. Others will prefer the type where you may be asked to imagine a beautiful place where you feel safe and comfortable or to imagine yourself floating on a cloud. These are backed up by positive suggestions about feeling calm, relaxed and happy. It is up to each individual to discover what suits them best. My first experience of relaxation was with a yoga teacher. We would do our yoga exercises for part of the evening and then finish up with relaxation in the form of guided fantasy. The teacher would make suggestions about floating away and feeling calm and happy. This is my favourite type of relaxation exercise and I usually feel wonderful after it. I do not respond particularly well to those types that work through relaxing the body. I practised yoga and this type of relaxation for a year during an extremely difficult period of my life and I am sure I would not have coped as well without it. Before I took up yoga I had felt emotionally out-of-control and quite panic stricken at times. Those yoga classes helped me to build up my strength. I vividly remember having a panic attack a few days after leaving my husband – I felt as if I could not breathe and was terrified. Then I remembered my yoga teacher's advice to breathe deeply – I did it a few times and the panic passed.

You will find that if you regularly practise relaxation for a period of a time the feelings of calm spread into your life and you will be better able to deal effectively/assertively with situations. I think relaxation is a good place to start, particularly if you tend to be a fairly tense, uptight sort of person. From there you may find you want, like I did, to move onto meditation.

MEDITATION

I firmly believe that meditation is the best thing that has ever happened to me. I have been practising it now for nearly six years and the benefits have been enormous. I cannot recommend it highly enough, both in terms of personal development and feelings of calm and peace. I actually learned how to meditate when I was doing yoga 11 years ago, but I disliked it intensely at that time. The way I was taught required that I sit in the Lotus position which I found extremely uncomfortable. I would spend the twenty minutes of meditation time feeling stiff, uncomfortable, and wishing the twenty minutes was over. It was not a peaceful, pleasant experience. I also found that instead of feeling better in my life outside the meditation time I was often feeling worse. I did not understand this and gave it up, not to return to it for another five years.

The reason I returned to it was because a friend of mine did a course in meditation and personal development. She was extremely impressed by the benefits she had gained. She had suffered quite severely from depression but since her meditation course her depression had disappeared altogether. Upon her recommendation I enrolled on the same meditation course. There were a number of things I liked about the way I was now being taught. One was the importance of being physically comfortable – we sat in straight chairs or could lie down. For many Westerners the Lotus position is not appropriate and is extremely uncomfortable. My new teachers stressed keeping the spine straight and feeling comfortable – that made me very happy! It is very important to find a way of meditating that suits you personally.

The feelings of emotional discomfort which accompany meditation from time to time were also explained. What I had been unable to understand with my previous experience of meditation became clear and I was able to then make an 'informed' decision about whether I was prepared to continue. My teachers claimed (and I accept) that the conscious mind is the tip of the iceberg, the unconscious lies beneath that, and beneath that lies a level of consciousness at which we are all joined. What happens in meditation is that we sink into the different levels of mind. Sometimes meditation is a wonderful experience where all sense of time disappears – I experience it as if I have been somewhere very deep and peaceful. At other times I find that my conscious mind is very active and I am continually bringing myself back to concentrating on my mantra (a sound which is used as a tool to shut out conscious thoughts). Sometimes I just do not want to do it and feel fidgety and restless while I do – I still do it at these times and remind myself of what the teachers said – 'The times you do not want to meditate are the times you need to meditate most'. The reason for the discomfort is that meditation puts us in touch with things that are buried in the unconscious mind. They are buried for a very good reason – we do not want to remember or deal with the experience since we put it there in the first place because it was too painful for us.

You may be thinking, 'What is the point of dredging up things from the past that were painful? Why not just leave them there? What is the point?' The point is that these painful memories and experiences affect us today. Because we do not remember does not mean that they do not influence our lives in the present. Many of the beliefs upon which we run our lives rest on decisions we made when we were very young about the way the world and people are. I remember one of my meditation lecturers saying, 'Would you let a two-year-old child run your car? Well, you are letting a two-year-old child run your life!' By this he meant that the way most of us run our lives is based on decisions we made at a very early age. To bring the situation and the decisions into conscious awareness means that we can then make new decisions as adults. One of the decisions I had made in early life was that standing up in front of a group of people was dangerous and terrifying. Six months after facing my fear about this, I was asked if I would teach assertion training – my immediate response was 'yes'. Three months later I was teaching – and loving it. Meditation can help you to work through and overcome fears that limit your capacity to be more of what you would like to be – and are capable of being.

Something else that meditation does is that it stabilizes you. I have found that there is a place inside me where I feel calm and at peace at *all* times, even when things are really rough. The past year has been an extremely difficult one for me – adjusting to life in England, grieving for my friends and for Australia, grieving over the death of my father three months after I arrived here, getting used to the pressures and demands of having family around me and being unemployed. I felt very low for a period of about eight months, but during this period I also felt calm and at peace in what I would call the 'centre of my being'. I was not the only one who was aware of this – I received feedback from a number of people that they also experienced me in this way. Meditation has given me a very strong 'core' which enables me to be calm in a storm and to develop into the person I want to be. This does not mean that I live in the future and am waiting for the time when I can be happy with myself. For the most part I am happy with myself now – and I also want to change. I can accept the present – and plan for the future.

Meditation and the peace and calm the practice of it brings, enables a person to relate assertively to others in a calm and relaxed way. My early attempts at assertion were often fraught with tension and this tension made me ineffective to a certain extent. Others often reacted to my tension because the effort to be assertive sometimes came across too forcefully and was seen as aggression. As I have calmed and relaxed myself, so my assertive skills have beome calm and relaxed. Behaving assertively does not have to be a 'heavy trip' – it can be light yet firm, effective yet relaxed.

A natural progression for me from meditation was to use my mind actively to create change. Relaxation is concerned with calming yourself while meditation is concerned with calming and developing a strong inner core plus bringing into awareness things from the past which prevent inner calm. The following sections deal with creating change in a more active, concentrated way.

AFFIRMATIONS

I wrote earlier in the book about Rational Emotive Therapy (See Chapter 11) and showed how it is not people or events that cause us to feel certain feelings, but *our* thoughts about the person or event. In discussing affirmations I am taking this a bit further to look at thoughts as being creative:

POSITIVE THOUGHTS CREATE POSITIVE RESULTS.
NEGATIVE THOUGHTS CREATE NEGATIVE RESULTS.

For example, if I keep telling myself often enough that I cannot do something, the result will be that I cannot do it. I can then turn the thought around to 'I can do it' and if I tell myself this often enough, the chances are that I will be able to do it.

Affirmations are concerned with changing negative thoughts (creating negative results) into positive thoughts (creating positive results). There are many books available on positive thinking and its power. You may have read some yourself, felt great about them and yourself for a short period of time, and then put them away deciding either they do not work or that it must be your fault that they do not work for you – further confirmation of your hopelessness as a person. Affirmations are about positive thinking, but not in the form 'read this book and your life will be changed – think different thoughts and like magic, a new person!' Affirmations do not concentrate only on the conscious mind, they work on the unconscious mind as well, creating change at a deep level. You have probably experienced many beliefs that you accept on the conscious level, but when it comes to your 'actual' behaviour it becomes apparent that you are unable to act on your beliefs. For example, when I was a student I believed on the conscious level that I was equal to my lecturers. However, in my behaviour it was quite apparent to me that I did not feel equal at all. My conscious and unconscious beliefs were not in alignment. Affirmations concentrate on bringing conscious and unconscious beliefs together so they are the same. When conscious and unconscious beliefs are different they work against each other – when they work together great things can be achieved.

There are a number of books available on affirmations, how to choose them and how to use them. Again, the problem with the books I have read on this subject is that they do not fully inform people of the process involved. This does not mean that the books are without value – I have a number of them on my bookshelves and I have found them extremely useful. However, I think that if I had learned about affirmations from these books, I would have decided very quickly that they do not work. Luckily I was first introduced to affirmations by my meditation teachers. I am now convinced that they do work, from my own experiences. I have found that affirmations are tougher to work through than they appear to be from books. I will first explain what they are and, secondly, how they work.

I said earlier that thoughts are creative. Affirmations are positive thoughts that you feed into your conscious and unconscious mind. I find a useful way of understanding the concept is to think of the mind as a computer. We have all had a great deal of information fed into our computers and, particularly during our formative years (0–7), much of that information was extremely negative. You have only to listen to parents talking to their children to hear the negatives – 'Don't do this', 'Don't touch that', 'You dirty girl', 'You nasty little boy', etc., etc. I am not intending to criticise parents – most of them repeat the things they heard as children. Parents are not the only ones who feed negative beliefs into children – teachers, priests, ministers and other adults and children do the same. Of course, we also get positive beliefs as well, but since they are not a problem I do not need to discuss them here. The messages I have discussed above are mainly to do with self-esteem, but we also receive other types of messages which can limit us as people. For example, if you are told often enough 'Be careful. Don't hurt yourself', you may grow up being very fearful and unable to take risks. Or if you are told 'Big boys don't cry', you may have great difficulty in feeling or expressing hurt or sadness.

Affirmations are used to counter and flush out negative beliefs. When I am using an affirmation I am feeding new information into my 'computer'. My experience of them is that when I start them they work wonderfully for a few days. For example, I did an affirmation on self-esteem – 'I, Beverley, am capable and lovable.' I felt great – I felt capable and lovable! I was very excited. 'It works', I thought. However, after a few days my feelings about myself were worse than before I started. Numerous negative thoughts about why I was not capable or lovable came streaming out. I felt miserable. At this point I would probably have given up and thought 'These affirmations do not work. I felt better about myself before I started'. What stopped me from giving up was that I had been warned this is exactly what would happen. I knew that the discomfort I was feeling did, in fact, mean that the affirmation was working.

When you feed the positive information into your mind it initially works because you are working on the superficial level of the mind. As you continue with the affirmation, the new positive information seeps through the deeper levels of mind – to the unconscious. In the unconscious reside beliefs about ourselves that we do not even know exist. The positive information meets the negative beliefs and forces them out into awareness. They do not come into awareness merely as intellectual ideas, there are feelings attached to them. This is the reason for the discomfort and the feeling that things seem worse than ever. Something I think is important to remember is that just because these beliefs and feelings are unconscious does not mean they are not affecting your life. They were the reason, in my case, that I did *not* feel capable and lovable. I brought them to the surface, processed them out, and then I felt capable and lovable.

There are a number of different ways to do affirmations, but there are certain rules which apply to them all:

- They should include your own name.
- They should always be spoken in the present tense – 'I, Beverley, am capable and lovable' *not* 'I, Beverley, want to be capable and lovable'.
- They should be spoken in the first, second *and* third person – 'I', 'You' *and* 'She/He'. The reason for this is that we have received different types of messages. For example, as a child you may have heard 'You are incapable' or 'She is unlovable'. You then turn it into 'I am not lovable – I am not capable'. Using the first, second *and* third person, counters *all* previous messages you may have received.

Affirmations can be said to yourself over and over again – repetition and persistence is the key. I tend to do them in the way I was originally taught – at the end of meditation for about five minutes. Having meditated I am in a very relaxed state and I have greater access to my unconscious mind. I also do them when I am out walking on my own. I should mention that I am saying them in my mind, not speaking them out loud! For one-third of my walk I say 'I' one-third 'you' and one-third 'she'. I have stuck them on my wall so they stay at the forefront of my mind and remind me to say them. I remember one time I was talking to a friend on the phone and she told me I was being very hard on myself and it would be a good idea if I wrote a big notice to stick on the wall saying 'I, Beverley, am being kind to myself!'. 'Silly', I thought. But I did it and it did make a difference.

Affirmations can also be written and many believe this is the most powerful type of affirmation. You take a sheet of paper, draw a line down the middle, write the affirmation on the lefthand side and on the right you write any negative thoughts that come into your mind:

Affirmation	Negative thought
I, Beverley, am capable and lovable.	No. I'm not.
I, Beverley, am capable and lovable.	Rubbish.
I, Beverley, am capable and lovable.	I wish I were.
I, Beverley, am capable and lovable.	Who am I fooling?

Affirmation	Negative thought
I, Beverley, am capable and lovable.	It is not true.
I, Beverley, am capable and lovable.	I would like to be.
I, Beverley, am capable and lovable.	Maybe I could be.
I, Beverley, am capable and lovable.	Perhaps it may be true.
You, Beverley, are capable and lovable.	Who says?
You, Beverley, are capable and lovable.	Are you joking?
You, Beverley, are capable and lovable.	Do you think so?
You, Beverley, are capable and lovable.	Well, I suppose I I am good at some things.
You, Beverley, are capable and lovable.	I would like to believe it.
She, Beverley, is capable and lovable.	No, she is not.

Affirmation	Negative thought
She, Beverley, is capable and lovable.	I think she is mean.
She, Beverley, is capable and lovable.	Some people like her.
She, Beverley, is capable and lovable.	She has many close friends.
She, Beverley, is capable and lovable.	Maybe there are some good points.

By doing it this way you can see the negative beliefs that get in the way of you feeling the way you would like to feel. You will notice how the thoughts change from very negative to less negative to hopeful. Eventually the negatives will be gone and positive beliefs will take their place. The old beliefs will not change overnight – it requires persistence and determination.

Affirmations can be used for self-esteem, relationships, health, weight, assertion, etc. Some possible affirmations related to assertion are:

I, ..., *have the right to say no.*
I, ..., *express my opinions easily.*
I, ..., *am becoming more assertive with each passing day.*
I, ..., *openly express my needs and feelings.*
I, ..., *treat myself and others with respect.*

There are many possible affirmations. I have found it best to find ones that feel totally comfortable for me. Look at the areas you find difficult, hear your negative

thoughts, then turn them into positive affirmations.
For example:

Negative – I am so hopeless the way I let my boss
walk over me.

Positive – I, . . ., am becoming stronger and more able
to express my needs with every passing day.

Affirmations involve the use of words (written or
spoken mentally) to make change. Another powerful
method of creating change using the mind is through
the use of creative visualization.

CREATIVE VISUALIZATION

Creative visualization is the process whereby you
visualize yourself in various situations the way you
would like to be. For example, I used visualization
techniques to improve my performance at interviews. I
imagined myself going into an interview and behaving
the way I wanted to behave in my mind. I saw myself
walk into the room with erect body posture, I
confidently shook hands with all the members of the
interview panel, I sat down and maintained a calm and
relaxed manner, I answered questions after giving
them some thought (I did not rush), at the end of the
interview I thanked them for their time and walked
out confidently. I visualized (imagined) this scene to
myself over and over again. My interview skills
improved quite dramatically over a short period of time
and I received feedback from interviewers to that
effect. I felt good about a particular interview and the
feedback confirmed that the panel were impressed by
my performance.

Creative visualization is not weird or strange, it is
something that we all do whether we realize it or not.
Unfortunately, we often use it negatively and against
our own best interests. For example, how often have
you catastrophized about something in the future –

imagined yourself failing, or making a fool of yourself – and it has happened. Much of this visualization process is unconscious and you may be quite unaware of how much you do it. Everything that has ever been created or invented was first an idea in someone's mind – it was visualized before coming into existence. If this is true, and I believe it is, then it stands to reason that you can use the process in a positive way to create success in your life and to create the person you want to be.

It is important to feel relaxed and comfortable when you are working with creative visualization – this appears to help in creating mental images. It seems that it is easier for some people to visualize than it is for others. I have found that my ability to visualize has improved over the years as I have used the technique – just like any other skill it has taken time and practice for me to see clearer pictures in my mind. It can be used in numerous ways and situations and I mention some books on page 143 to help with this if you want to look into it further.

You can use creative visualization to improve your assertion skills. If there is someone you find it difficult to say no to, imagine doing it and see yourself handling the situation in the way you want to. Or, if you would like to be able to express your opinion in a group, see yourself doing it and the others in the group listening to you. Perhaps you would like to express love and caring with those who are dear to you – visualize yourself doing so. You can be what you want to be.

The four areas I have covered in this chapter are all aids to assertion. Relaxation and meditation will help you feel calmer in your assertion, affirmations and creative visualization will help create the changes you want at a deep and significant level of mind.

15.
WHERE TO FROM HERE?

So now you have read the book. You may have learned some things about assertion and the way to become assertive – I hope that you have. I hope also that you will see this book only as a beginning and that you will move onto other things to help in your development. I said at the beginning that this book was in no way intended as a substitute for an assertiveness training course. I recommend that you enrol in a course to learn more about it and, most importantly, to share your learning with others. Many people in my classes have said that one of the major things they had gained from the course was to discover that they were not alone – that others have the same difficulties in relating to people in an honest and meaningful way.

People sometimes get the impression that the only people who come to assertiveness training classes are shy and timid. It is true that some are, but there are many others who are outgoing and quite vocal. People come for numerous reasons. Some have lost their confidence – like women who have spent many years at home with children or men who have work problems. Many come because of broken relationships; others are in relationships that they would like to save before it is too late. Others have been promoted to supervisory positions and want to learn the people skills they have never been taught. Some want to be promoted and think better communication skills will help their performance at interviews and on the job. Many have jobs which involve people and they want to be more effective in communicating with them – doctors, dentists, teachers, civil servants, waiters, shop assistants, lawyers, secretaries, etc. In one of my classes I had a management consultant who was also a competent and experienced public speaker. A member of the group asked him why he was there since he seemed so self-assured and assertive. His reply was 'I have no trouble speaking to 200 people, but when it comes down to one, I do not know how to communicate'.

It is the wide range of ages and types of people I work with, which makes teaching assertiveness training such a fascinating experience for me. I like to teach mixed groups because I think this is an accurate representation of what happens in the real world. We do not live in a world made up solely of men or women. However, for some people it is appropriate to choose a class which is single-sexed. Many women feel intimidated in a group with men and for them it may be wiser to choose a women's group. There are groups available for women only. There are also mixed groups available if this is what you would prefer. I have not heard of any groups for men only, but this does not mean they do not exist. It is a matter of doing some research yourself to see what you can find. Adult education centres are a good place to start – if they do not run them, perhaps you can take an assertive step and ask them to put one on!

There are other types of communications courses available and it maybe worthwhile trying some of these. I have done numerous different types of communications courses and while there have been a few that I have not liked or found useful, I have gained something from most of them. They have helped to reinforce and sometimes put a different perspective on things I have already learned. Again, it is a matter of doing some research and finding what you feel is most suitable for you. Also, one thing leads to another – enrol in one course and you will undoubtedly hear about other things through it.

Relaxation and meditation are areas I recommend

pursuing for reasons already outlined in Chapter 14. I think it is better to take a course and learn how to do them properly with the support of a group. I meditate twice a day for twenty minutes morning and evening. This requires that you discipline yourself and I found that the support and encouragement of the teacher and the group enabled me to get into a routine – and then stick to it when the group was no longer there. Many yoga teachers will instruct you in meditation, but may ask you to adopt uncomfortable positions, though if you are supple and flexible this may not be a problem for you.

At the end of this book I have listed books that I have learned and gained from. I have put them into different categories to enable you to choose more easily. I cannot recommend strongly enough that you read some of them to reinforce what you have discovered in this book and perhaps in the courses you decide to take.

And last but not least – set yourself some goals. Decide where you want to go and what you want to be – by doing this you are on your way. Write them down – make them concrete and clear. A life without goals and direction is like getting on a plane to an unknown destination. Know where you are going, but be prepared to deviate at times because the detour may be necessary to get you where you want to go. Be flexible *and* do not set your goals in concrete – *trust!*

There is not much left that I want to say now, except to wish you well with assertion, your personal development and your life. I hope you have found this book useful and that it has had some meaning for you. I hope also that you will decide to pursue the ideas in this book further – either now or in the future. As I said in the Introduction, I believe a world in which people are more in touch with their feelings and able to communicate honestly with each other would be a better world. It is my desire that this book will make a contribution towards creating that better world for us all.

FURTHER READING

ASSERTION

The Assertive Option, P. Jakubowski and A. Lange,
  Research Press, 1978
Self-Assertion for Women, P.E. Butler, Harper & Row,
  1981
Your Perfect Right, R.E. Alberti and M.L. Emmons,
  Impact Publishers, 1982
A Woman In your Own Right, A. Dickson, Quartet
  Books, 1982

BODY LANGUAGE

Body Language, J. Fast, Pan Books, 1971
Body Language, A. Pease, Camel Publishing Co, 1981

SELF-TALK

A New Guide to Rational Living, A. Ellis and R.A.
  Harper, Wilshire Book Co, 1978
A Conscious Person's Guide to Relationships, K. Keyes,
  Living Love Publications, 1979

RELAXATION

The Relaxation Response, H. Benson, Avon
  Publications, 1966

MEDITATION

Journey of Awakening, R. Dass, Bantam Books, 1978

AFFIRMATIONS

You Can Heal Your Life, L.L. Hay, Hay House, 1984
I Deserve Love, S. Ray, Celestial Arts, 1982
Loving Relationships, S. Ray, Celestial Arts, 1980
The Only Diet There Is, S. Ray, Celestial Arts, 1981

CREATIVE VISUALIZATION

Creative Visualization, S. Gawain, Bantam Books, 1982
Living in the Light, S. Gawain, Whatever Publishing,
    1986
The Fantasy Factor, H.E. Stanton, Macdonald Optima,
    1988

SELF UNDERSTANDING

Why Am I Afraid To Tell You Who I Am?, J. Powell,
    Argus Communications, 1969
On Becoming A Person (A Therapist's View of
    Psychotherapy), C. Rogers, Constable & Co, 1967

The following titles are also available from Vermilion.
To order your copy direct (p+p free), use the form below or
call our credit-card hotline on **01279 427203**.

Please send me

...... copies of **ALL IN THE MIND?** by Brian Roet @ £8.99

...... copies of **PERSONAL THERAPY** by Brian Roet @ £8.99

...... copies of **SEX: HOW TO MAKE IT BETTER FOR
BOTH OF YOU** by Martin Cole & Windy Dryden @ £8.99

...... copies of **PANIC ATTACKS** by Sue Breton @ £8.99

...... copies of **ANXIETY AND DEPRESSION** by Professor
Robert Priest @ £8.99

...... copies of **DIY PSYCHOTHERAPY** by Dr Martin
Shepherd @ £8.99

Mr/Ms/Mrs/Miss/Other (Block Letters)

....

Address..

....

....

Postcode...............................Signed...................................

HOW TO PAY

☐ I enclose a cheque/postal order for

£................................. made payable to 'Vermilion'

☐ I wish to pay by Access/Visa card (delete where
appropriate)

Card Number ☐☐☐☐☐☐☐☐☐☐☐☐☐☐☐☐☐☐☐

Expiry Date ☐☐☐☐

Post order to **Murlyn Services Ltd, PO Box 50, Harlow,
Essex CM17 ODZ.**

POSTAGE AND PACKING ARE FREE. Offer open in Great
Britain including Northern Ireland. Books should arrive less
than 28 days after we receive your order; they are subject to
availability at time of ordering. If not entirely satisfied return
in the same packaging and condition as received with a
covering letter within 7 days. Vermilion books are available
from all good booksellers.